# THEORY OF INDIVIDUATION

## A GUIDE TO JUNGIAN PSYCHOLOGY

# TABLE OF CONTENTS

# INTRODUCTION TO JUNGIAN PSYCHOLOGY

## Overview of Jungian Psychology

Jungian psychology, developed by Carl Gustav Jung, offers a comprehensive framework for understanding the human psyche and its dynamics. At its core, Jungian psychology explores the depths of the unconscious mind, delving into the dimensions of archetypes, the collective unconscious, and the process of individuation. This psychological paradigm acknowledges the importance of spirituality, mythology, and symbolism in shaping an individual's inner world, recognizing the interplay between cultural, societal, and personal influences.

Central to Jungian psychology is the concept of the psyche as a complex system comprising conscious and unconscious elements. It proposes that the human experience extends beyond mere rationality, encompassing deeper layers of the mind that hold profound symbolic and mythological significance. Through this holistic lens, the psyche is viewed as a dynamic tapestry of forces, motivations, and patterns that shape an individual's thoughts, behaviors, and emotions.

One of the fundamental tenets of Jungian psychology is the notion of archetypes, which are universal symbols and motifs that permeate human experiences across different cultures and historical epochs. These archetypal images, such as the hero, the shadow, the anima/animus, and the wise old man, are deeply ingrained in the collective unconscious and exert a powerful influence on human consciousness. By recognizing and engaging with these archetypes, individuals can gain insights into their own psychic makeup, facilitating a deeper understanding of themselves and others.

Jungian psychology introduces the concept of the collective unconscious, postulating that there exists a shared reservoir of inherited psychological material that transcends individual experiences. This collective unconscious encompasses universal themes, motifs, and symbols that underpin humanity's myths, legends, and cultural narratives. In exploring the depths of the collective unconscious, individuals may confront primal energies, ancestral memories, and timeless truths that resonate across diverse cultures and civilizations.

The framework also places significant emphasis on the process of individuation, which entails the realization of one's true self and the integration of disparate aspects of the psyche into a harmonious whole. Individuation involves a journey of self-discovery, self-acceptance, and self-transcendence, enabling individuals to achieve a more authentic and fulfilling existence. By embarking on the path of individuation, individuals strive to cultivate a balanced relationship between the conscious and unconscious dimensions of their being, leading to greater wholeness and psychological well-being.

**Central Concepts and Theoretical Underpinnings**

Jungian psychology is grounded in several central concepts and theoretical underpinnings that shape its understanding of the human psyche. At the core of Jung's framework is the notion of the collective unconscious, a reservoir of shared psychic material inherited from ancestral experience. This concept marks a departure from traditional psychological perspectives and serves as a foundational pillar in Jung's theories. In addition, the idea of archetypes, universal symbols and motifs present in the collective unconscious, forms another keystone in Jungian psychology. These archetypes, such as the shadow, anima/animus, and the self, provide a framework for understanding and interpreting the deep layers of the human psyche. Moreover, the theory of individuation, the lifelong process of integrating the various parts of the self to achieve wholeness, is a fundamental construct in Jungian psychology. Understanding the connections between the conscious and unconscious domains is essential to appreciating the holistic approach advocated by Jung. Furthermore, the significance of dreams, myths, and symbols as expressions of the unconscious mind cannot be overlooked in this context. These elements play a pivotal role in Jungian psychology, offering insights into the workings of the human psyche and facilitating the process of individuation. The emphasis on the transcendent function and the transformative potential of psychological conflicts adds depth to Jung's framework.

### The Role of the Psyche in Human Experience

The understanding of the psyche forms the foundation upon which individuation is built. The psyche encompasses the totality of the human mind, including both the conscious and unconscious elements. In Jungian terms, the psyche is not limited to individual experience but also encompasses the collective unconscious, which is shared among all individuals within a culture or society. Understanding the role of the psyche in human experience involves delving into the complexities of human cognition, emotion, and behavior.

At the core of Jungian psychology is the belief that the psyche plays a significant role in shaping human experience, influencing thoughts, feelings, and actions. According to Jung, the psyche is not just an accumulation of personal experiences but is also influenced by inherited or archetypal elements. These archetypes are universal symbols and themes that form the collective unconscious and can manifest in various forms such as myths, dreams, and cultural symbols. Therefore, the role of the psyche extends beyond individual experiences, encompassing a broader, interconnected web of human consciousness and experience.

The psyche's role in human experience is dynamic and transformative. Jungian psychology emphasizes the continuous interaction between the conscious and unconscious aspects of the psyche, shaping an individual's perceptions of self, others, and the world. Through its complex interplay, the psyche drives the processes of self-discovery, personal growth, and individuation. Understanding this relationship between the psyche and human experience provides profound insights into the nature of consciousness, identity formation, and the developmental trajectory of individuals.

The symbolic representations and manifestations of the psyche in human experience hold valuable insights into the underlying motivations, conflicts, and potentials within individuals. By exploring the depths of the psyche, individuals can gain a deeper understanding of their own patterns of behavior, emotional responses, and interpersonal dynamics. This exploration opens pathways for self-reflection and introspection, fostering a greater awareness of the interconnectedness between the personal and collective dimensions of human experience.

**Archetypes - The Building Blocks of the Unconscious**

Archetypes, as proposed by Carl Jung, form the fundamental components of the collective unconscious, playing a pivotal role in shaping human behavior, emotions, and thought patterns. These universal symbols and motifs are deeply embedded in the psyche of individuals, transcending cultural and historical boundaries. Jung's concept of archetypes originated from his extensive study of mythologies, folklore, and dreams, wherein he identified recurring images and themes that seemed to manifest across various human societies and ages.

At the core of the archetype theory is the idea that these primordial images are inherited and shared by all humanity, serving as cognitive templates that influence our perceptions and responses to the world. For instance, the archetype of the 'hero' embodies notions of courage, resilience, and the journey towards self-discovery, resonating with individuals irrespective of their societal backgrounds or personal experiences. Similarly, the 'mother' archetype encompasses nurturing and caregiving qualities, symbolizing the ideals of compassion and unconditional love.

Archetypes not only manifest in individual psyches but also permeate cultural expressions such as art, literature, and religious symbolism. Through this lens, analyzing archetypes becomes crucial in comprehending the deeper layers of human expression and creativity, shedding light on the profound connections between the conscious mind and the collective unconscious. By recognizing the archetypal motifs present in artistic endeavors, one can unravel the symbolic language that communicates universal truths and human experiences.

In the field of psychology, the concept of archetypes holds immense significance, offering a framework for understanding the recurring patterns observed in human behavior and relationships. By recognizing the archetypal dynamics at play within an individual's psyche, therapists can gain valuable insights into their clients' thought processes, motivations, and emotional struggles, thus informing more holistic and effective therapeutic interventions.

It is important to note that while archetypes provide a foundational understanding of the collective unconscious, their manifestations can vary widely among individuals due to personal experiences and environmental influences. This nuanced interplay between universal archetypes and individualized expressions presents a rich landscape for psychological exploration.

### The Significance of the Collective Unconscious

The concept of the collective unconscious represents a foundational pillar within Jungian psychology and holds immense significance in shaping human experience. Unlike the personal unconscious, which comprises an individual's unique repressed thoughts and memories, the collective unconscious delves into a shared reservoir of universal experiences and archetypal symbols that are common to all humanity. Jung proposed that this collective aspect of the unconscious is inherited and forms the backdrop for our individual experiences and behaviors.

At the core of the collective unconscious lie archetypes – primordial images and patterns that serve as universal symbols across cultures and epochs. These archetypes, such as the mother, the hero, the shadow, and the anima/animus, embody fundamental human experiences and emotions. They act as psychic instincts, influencing our perceptions, thoughts, and behaviors without our conscious awareness. By recognizing these archetypal motifs, individuals gain insights into their deeper motivations and psychological functioning.

The collective unconscious also underlines the interconnectedness of human experiences and emphasizes the universality of certain themes and symbols. It suggests that beyond cultural and temporal differences, there exist fundamental aspects of the human psyche that bind individuals together through a shared symbolic language. This notion has profound implications for fields such as literature, mythology, religion, and art, as it points to the recurring themes and motifs that echo throughout human expression, transcending boundaries of time and place.

The collective unconscious offers a framework for understanding the myths and folktales found across diverse cultures. Jung believed that these narratives reflect the universal themes and archetypes present in the collective unconscious, thereby serving as valuable sources of insight into the human condition. Through the exploration of myths and dreams, individuals can connect with the collective wisdom encoded in these symbolic expressions, leading to greater self-awareness and personal growth.

In clinical practice, recognition of the collective unconscious and its archetypal manifestations enables therapists to comprehend the deep-seated sources of their patients' conflicts and aspirations. By integrating the collective unconscious into therapeutic approaches, psychologists can help individuals move towards self-realization and individuation. The acknowledgment of these shared symbols and archetypal motifs provides a sense of connection and validation, fostering a deeper understanding of one's own psychological landscape and facilitating the integration of unconscious material.

### Individuation

Individuation, as conceptualized by Carl Jung, represents a profound psychological evolution that transcends mere personal development. At its core, individuation encapsulates the process of integrating and harmonizing the disparate elements of the psyche to achieve wholeness and self-realization. This transformative journey encompasses the unfolding of an individual's unique potential and the actualization of their authentic identity. Grounded in the belief that each person carries within them inherent resources for growth and fulfillment, individuation serves as a guiding framework for traversing the complexities of human existence. Through this lens, individuals are invited to embark on a deeply introspective and introspective quest, fusing the wisdom of introspection with the vistas of external experience. The journey of individuation is not a linear path nor a destination to be reached; instead, it embodies an ongoing, cyclical process of self-discovery and integration. As one delves deeper into the labyrinthine recesses of the unconscious, confronting latent aspects of the self and engaging with archetypal energies, they necessarily undergo a complex unfolding of their inner world. This inner alchemy brings forth a heightened awareness and understanding, enabling individuals to confront and reconcile opposing forces within themselves. Crucially, the concept of individuation distinguishes itself from traditional Freudian perspectives by emphasizing the transcendence of personal conflicts and traumas to unlock the reservoirs of creativity and resilience residing within the psyche. While Freud's focus predominantly centered on the resolution of neuroses and repressed desires, Jung's individuation propounds a broader, more holistic perspective that encompasses spiritual, cultural, and existential dimensions. Embracing the dynamic interplay between conscious and unconscious processes, individuation invites individuals to engage in a profound dialogue with their innermost selves, shedding light on aspects of the psyche that have long remained obscured. Through this transformative process, individuals are empowered to embrace their unique authenticity and contribute meaningfully to the collective tapestry of humanity.

### Individuation vs. Traditional Freudian Perspectives

In understanding the concept of individuation, it is essential to compare and contrast it with traditional Freudian perspectives. Sigmund Freud, known as the father of psychoanalysis, proposed a theory of personality development that heavily influenced the field of psychology. Freud's focus on the role of the unconscious mind and early childhood experiences in shaping an individual's psyche laid the groundwork for his theories of psychosexual development, defense mechanisms, and the structure of the mind—particularly the id, ego, and superego.

One of the primary distinctions between Jung's concept of individuation and traditional Freudian perspectives lies in their approach to the unconscious. While Freud emphasized the influence of repressed desires and unresolved conflicts on human behavior, Jung expanded this view to incorporate the collective unconscious and archetypes. In doing so, he broadened the scope of the unconscious to include universal symbols and images that are shared across cultures and generations, offering a deeper understanding of the human experience.

Freud's emphasis on the resolution of sexual and aggressive impulses as the driving force behind personality development contrasts with Jung's broader view of individuation as a journey toward self-realization and wholeness. Where Freudian psychology often focused on addressing psychological disorders and resolving internal conflicts, Jungian psychology aimed at achieving a more profound integration of the various components of the psyche.

Another significant difference lies in the portrayal of the self. For Freud, the ego plays a central role in mediating between the demands of the id, superego, and external reality, while Jung expanded the concept of the self to encompass the striving for personal growth, meaning, and purpose. This holistic approach in Jungian psychology shifts the focus from conflict resolution to the realization of one's potential and the actualization of the self.

Despite these differences, it is important to note that both Freudian and Jungian perspectives have contributed to the field of psychology. While Freud's work continues to influence therapeutic approaches and our understanding of the human psyche, Jung's elaboration on individuation provides a comprehensive framework for personal development and spiritual growth.

## Cognitive and Emotional Dimensions of Individuation

The process of individuation involves a profound exploration of the unconscious mind, delving into the cognitive and emotional undercurrents shaping an individual's psyche. As individuals embark on their journey towards wholeness and self-realization, they are confronted with a myriad of cognitive challenges, including confronting repressed thoughts and acknowledging suppressed emotions. This introspective examination of the psyche requires a synthesis of the cognitive and emotional spheres, as one seeks to integrate the disparate and often conflicting elements of the self. The cognitive dimension of individuation involves unraveling the complex web of thoughts, beliefs, and perceptions that shape one's understanding of the world and oneself. It necessitates a critical assessment of the conscious mind's constructs and an exploration of underlying cognitive patterns, conditioning, and biases. Furthermore, this cognitive aspect of individuation entails an intellectual grappling with archetypal symbols and their significance in personal meaning-making, fostering a deeper comprehension of one's psychological landscape. Alongside the cognitive dimension, the emotional facet of individuation plays a pivotal role in the transformative process. Unearthing deep-seated emotions, traumas, and unresolved conflicts demands a profound emotional resilience and introspective courage. Individuals are required to trverse the labyrinth of their emotional experiences, embracing both the light and shadow aspects of their psyche. Embracing emotional vulnerability and authenticity becomes paramount as individuals traverse the tumultuous terrain of individuation. Moreover, the integration of cognitive and emotional dimensions is facilitated through various therapeutic modalities and self-reflective practices such as dream analysis, active imagination, and creative expression. These avenues serve as conduits for reconciling cognitive insights with emotional realities, further nurturing the individuation process.

# THE GENESIS OF INDIVIDUATION

## Early Psychological Theories and Their Influence on Jung

Influenced by early psychological theories, Jung's divergence from prevailing schools of thought, particularly his departure from Sigmund Freud's psychoanalytic framework, laid the groundwork for the development of his own distinctive concepts. At the heart of these influences lies a fundamental departure from the reductionist and deterministic aspects of mainstream psychological theories prevalent during Jung's era. Early psychological theories, such as behaviorism and structuralism, sought to explain human behavior and cognition through observable behaviors or mental structures. Meanwhile, the pervasive influence of positivism and materialism in scientific exploration had far-reaching implications for the understanding of the human mind. Distinctly, Jung's exposure to these foundational concepts sparked intellectual inquiry and introspection, triggering a deliberate departure from the deterministic paradigms that underpinned early psychological theories. Rather than framing human experience within rigid confines, Jung's subsequent explorations delved deep into the symbols, myths, and archetypes that constituted the individual psyche, paving the way for his pioneering theories on individuation.

## Jung's Departure from Freud

As Jung's ideas began to form and evolve, a schism emerged between him and his former mentor, Sigmund Freud. This ideological parting of ways marked a pivotal moment not only in the trajectories of these two influential figures but also in the course of psychological theory as a whole. At the heart of this divergence lay fundamental differences in their philosophical underpinnings and theoretical frameworks.

While Freud's emphasis on the primacy of the sexual and aggressive instincts in shaping human behavior was well-established, Jung crystallized a different perspective centered around the broader concept of the collective unconscious and archetypes. This departure signified a shift from a narrow focus on repressed desires to a more expansive exploration of universal symbols and mythological motifs that transcend individual experiences.

The contrast between Freud's emphasis on the significance of the Oedipus complex and Jung's development of the concept of individuation epitomized the philosophical rift. Freud's revolutionary work on the structures of the psyche was foundational, but Jung's divergent approach posited a more holistic and inclusive understanding of the human psyche that transcended purely sexual and aggressive drives.

In addition to their theoretical discrepancies, their personal relationship also played a significant role in their parting. As their friendship evolved into a professional collaboration, tensions arose due to differences in temperament and divergent professional ambitions. This personal discord ultimately culminated in Jung's resignation from his position within the psychoanalytic community, marking a definitive break from the Freudian circle.

### The Evolution of Jung's Thought Processes

Jung's early engagement with psychiatry and neurology, particularly during his tenure at the Burghölzli psychiatric hospital, served as the crucible for the inception of his revolutionary ideas. Influenced by the emerging fields of psychoanalysis and anthropology, Jung embarked on a scholarly quest marked by intellectual curiosity and empirical rigor.

One pivotal milestone in the evolution of Jung's thought was his exploration of the collective unconscious and archetypes, which germinated through intensive introspection and cross-cultural studies. This paradigm-shifting endeavor laid the foundation for his conceptualization of individuation and the symbolic manifestations of the psyche. Moreover, Jung's experiences with prominent cultural traditions and mythologies steered the trajectory of his cognitive framework, enriching his understanding of the human condition and deepening his appreciation for the universality of psychological phenomena.

As Jung delved into the complexities of alchemy, religion, and mysticism, he endeavored to synthesize diverse philosophical threads, giving rise to a tapestry of ideas that transcended temporal and disciplinary boundaries. His voracious appetite for knowledge compelled him to venture into esoteric realities, seeking insights from the wisdom traditions of various civilizations. The amalgamation of these multifaceted influences catalyzed a paradigmatic shift in Jung's cognitive architecture, leading to the formulation of seminal theories that continue to reverberate across the sphere of modern psychology.

In tandem with this metamorphosis, Jung's engagement with patients and his introspective self-analysis facilitated the crystallization of his theoretical constructs. Endowed with an empathic demeanor and an unwavering commitment to understanding the nuances of the human psyche, Jung harnessed his clinical encounters as profound sources of inspiration and empirical validation. Through rigorous self-reflection and meticulous documentation of his own psychic experiences, Jung traversed the labyrinthine corridors of the unconscious, elucidating the enigmatic aspects of human consciousness and elucidating the pathways toward individuation.

### Cultural and Intellectual Influences During Jung's Era

During the time of Carl Jung, the late 19th and early 20th centuries witnessed a period of significant cultural and intellectual upheaval. This era, often referred to as the fin de siècle or the 'turn of the century', was characterized by unprecedented shifts in societal values, artistic expression, and scientific inquiry. One of the most profound influences on Jung's thinking was the burgeoning field of psychoanalysis pioneered by Sigmund Freud, whose revolutionary ideas were challenging conventional views on human behavior and the nature of the mind. Additionally, the rapid advancements in technology, industrialization, and urbanization led to profound changes in the way people lived and interacted with their environment. This transformative period fostered an atmosphere of curiosity, skepticism, and a thirst for understanding the human experience. Moreover, the prevalence of spiritualism, occultism, and the exploration of non-Western philosophies contributed to a rich tapestry of belief systems and alternative worldviews, all of which played a role in shaping Jung's receptivity to diverse cultural influences. The juxtaposition of traditional, conservative ideals with emerging avant-garde movements contributed to a cultural tension that challenged established norms and perceptions. The enduring impact of the Romantic movement, with its emphasis on individuality, imagination, and emotional expression, further cultivated an environment ripe for introspection and self-discovery. Artistic movements such as symbolism, surrealism, and expressionism also permeated the collective consciousness, reflecting a deep-seated longing for transcendence and catharsis, themes that would resonate deeply with Jung's exploration of the human psyche. Furthermore, the emergence of comparative mythology and the study of ancient religions provided Jung with a wealth of archetypal symbols and narratives that would later become integral to his theory of the collective unconscious.

## The Role of Symbolism in Shaping Jung's Ideas

Symbolism, within the context of individuation, refers to the use of tangible or abstract representations that carry deeper, often unconscious, meanings and serve as conduits for the expression of archetypal forces. Jung postulated that symbols are critical vehicles through which the unconscious communicates with the conscious mind, providing insight into an individual's psyche and facilitating the process of self-discovery.

Jung observed that throughout history and across cultures, symbols have played a pivotal role in spiritual and psychological contexts. Whether found in religious rites, folklore, dreams, or myths, symbols act as gateways to the collective unconscious, transcending individual experiences to tap into universal human themes. The enduring nature of certain symbols, such as the mandala, the serpent, or the hero's journey, led Jung to conclude that these archetypal motifs held profound psychological significance and were rooted in the collective human experience.

Jung emphasized that the interpretation of symbols should not be approached with a fixed, universal understanding; rather, he advocated for a personalized, introspective analysis that acknowledges the specific cultural and personal context of the individual. The incorporation of symbols into therapeutic practices, particularly in analytical psychology, aims to illuminate the unconscious dynamics at play within an individual, enabling the exploration of unconscious material that may be obstructing the path toward individuation.

In examining the relevance of symbols, Jung delved into the transformative power inherent in engaging with symbolic imagery. He posited that the process of engaging with symbols—be it through active imagination, dream analysis, or artistic expression—could promote an integration of the disparate elements of the psyche, foster self-awareness, and guide individuals towards achieving a state of wholeness. This transformative potential underscores the profound impact that symbols can exert on the psychological well-being and development of an individual.

The profundity of symbolism is manifested most tangibly in Jung's own body of work, where he extensively utilized symbol-laden concepts such as the anima/animus, the shadow, and the persona to elucidate the complexities of the human psyche and the individuation process. These formulations provided practitioners and scholars with a rich framework for interpreting the interplay between conscious and unconscious elements, inviting them to explore the depths of the psyche through the symbological lens.

## Foundational Texts

From the groundbreaking 'Psychological Types' to his explorations on archetypes in 'Archetypes and the Collective Unconscious,' Jung's writings serve as the cornerstone upon which the edifice of individuation theory is erected. Through his analysis of myths, symbols, and dreams, Jung elucidates the profound connection between the individual psyche and the universal symbolic patterns ingrained in cultures throughout history. Additionally, 'The Psychology of the Transference' provides an authoritative understanding of the transferential relationship between therapist and patient, shedding light on the dynamics of the unconscious. Beyond his own oeuvre, Jung's engagement with alchemical texts and Eastern philosophies enriches his discourse, emphasizing the universality of the individuation process transcending cultural boundaries. Furthermore, a critical examination of the Red Book—Jung's personal compendium of fantasies and reflections—provides insight into the deeply introspective and visionary aspects of his individuation journey.

## The Seeds of Individuation in Ancient Philosophical Traditions

The philosophical traditions of various cultures such as India, China, Greece, and Egypt contain implicit understandings of the individual's journey towards self-realization and integration. In the Indian philosophical tradition, particularly within the traditions of Hinduism and Buddhism, the idea of an individual's quest for self-discovery is central to the concept of moksha or nirvana. Similarly, in Chinese philosophy, the Taoist notion of achieving harmony with the natural order echoes the goal of integrating conflicting elements within the self, a principle fundamental to individuation. The ancient Greeks also contemplated the notion of individuation, with philosophers such as Plato and Aristotle exploring the nature of the self and its connection to the greater cosmos. Their inquiries into the pursuit of virtue, wisdom, and knowledge bear striking resemblance to the aims of individuation as envisioned by Jung. Additionally, the mystical traditions of ancient Egypt delved into the mysteries of the soul's journey and transformation, offering insights into the archetypal motifs that continue to resonate in Jungian psychology today. The groundwork for individuation was being laid millennia ago and highlight the universality of humankind's search for self-realization and wholeness.

# CORE PRINCIPLES AND POSTULATES

## Archetypes - Universal Symbols and Their Significance

1. Historical Perspectives:

Humanity's fascination with archetypal symbols can be traced back to antiquity, where various cultures and civilizations found significance in recurring motifs and universal patterns. The ancient Egyptians, for instance, revered deities and mythical figures that embodied archetypal traits such as wisdom, power, and transformation. Similarly, the Greek pantheon, with its gods and goddesses representing archetypal forces like love, war, and wisdom, provided a rich tapestry of symbolic expressions that influenced art, literature, and philosophy. As civilization progressed, archetypal imagery continued to permeate cultural narratives, from the heroic epics of the Mesopotamians and the Indian subcontinent to the mystic traditions of the Far East.

The concept of archetypes also found resonance in the domain of philosophy, where thinkers like Plato and Aristotle pondered the existence of ideal forms and universal principles underlying reality. Their contemplations on timeless essences and transcendent ideals echoed the archetypal themes that would later be identified by psychologists and scholars in the modern era. Furthermore, the medieval period witnessed the allegorical interpretations of religious texts, revealing an inherent understanding of archetypal symbolism within sacred stories and parables.

In the early modern period, the burgeoning field of psychology saw glimpses of archetypal theories emerging in the works of thinkers like Carl Gustav Carus and Gustav Fechner, who explored the collective unconscious and the deep layers of the human psyche. However, it was not until the pioneering work of Swiss psychiatrist Carl Gustav Jung in the 20th century that the concept of archetypes was formally articulated and integrated into psychological discourse. Jung's extensive study of mythology, religion, and cross-cultural symbolism culminated in his elucidation of archetypal patterns and their profound impact on human behavior, dreams, and creativity.

2. Conceptual Framework:

The conceptual framework of archetypes elucidates the collective unconscious's reservoir of universal symbols and patterns that underpin human experience. Central to this framework is the notion that archetypes are innate, inherited predispositions that mold an individual's perceptions, emotions, and behavior, transcending cultural and temporal boundaries. At the core of this framework lies the understanding that archetypes serve as primordial blueprints that inform and shape an individual's psyche, representing essential themes and motifs common to all humanity.

When delving into the conceptual framework of archetypes, it becomes evident that these universal symbols manifest in diverse forms and manifestations, often assuming personas such as the Hero, the Mother, the Shadow, and the Trickster, among others. These archetypal constructs hold profound significance, as they encapsulate fundamental aspects of the human condition, elucidating existential dilemmas, psychological conflicts, and transformative journeys. Furthermore, the framework emphasizes that archetypes operate on both personal and collective levels, permeating individual psyches while also reverberating through cultural narratives and myths, thereby shaping societal norms and beliefs.

Within this conceptual framework, archetypes are understood as dynamic and evolving forces that continually influence human development and self-discovery. They imbue life with layers of meaning and symbolism, fueling creative expression, religious rituals, and artistic representations throughout history. Additionally, the framework recognizes that individuals may resonate with certain archetypal patterns more strongly than others, leading to diverse personal mythologies and narrative constructions. This recognition invites an exploration of the interplay between individual experiences and the vast tapestry of collective archetypal imagery.

An integral facet of the conceptual framework is the comprehension of how archetypes shape not only personal identity but also interpersonal dynamics. By recognizing archetypal influences in relationships, familial structures, and societal institutions, individuals gain insights into the underlying symbolic forces that govern human interactions. This understanding fosters empathy, tolerance, and a deeper appreciation for the complexities inherent in the human experience, ultimately contributing to a more nuanced and enriched social fabric.

In essence, comprehending the conceptual framework of archetypes entails embracing the depth and breadth of human consciousness, acknowledging the pervasive influence of universal symbols, and recognizing the profound impact of archetypal patterns on individual and collective psyches. It beckons us to embark on an introspective journey that explores the profound resonance of archetypes in their lives, fostering a deeper understanding of ourselves and the interconnectedness of the human experience.

3. Major Archetypal Constructs:

Major Archetypal Constructs, often described as 'primordial images,' encompass a wide spectrum of symbolic patterns that shape individual and collective consciousness. Among these constructs are the Persona, Shadow, Anima/Animus, the Wise Old Man, the Hero, the Mother, the Child, and the Self. Each archetype embodies universal aspects of the human psyche, shedding light on profound dimensions of the human condition. The Persona archetype encapsulates the social mask an individual wears in the outer world, serving as a protective shield against societal demands. Conversely, the Shadow archetype represents the repressed and unconscious aspects of the psyche, containing elements deemed unacceptable by the conscious mind. The Anima/Animus archetype personifies the contrasexual qualities within individuals, revealing the feminine and masculine energies residing within the psyche. The Wise Old Man archetype signifies wisdom, knowledge, and guidance, often associated with mentorship and spiritual insight. The Hero archetype embodies the courageous and transformative journey of self-discovery and overcoming adversity. The Mother archetype symbolizes nurturance, compassion, and fertility, representing the nurturing and life-giving aspects of existence. Similarly, the Child archetype embodies innocence, spontaneity, and the potential for growth and creativity, reflecting the primal and unconditioned aspects of the self. Lastly, the Self archetype represents the center of the psyche, epitomizing wholeness, integration, and the realization of one's true identity. Understanding and integrating these archetypal constructs are central to Jungian individuation, as they provide a roadmap for traversing the complexities of the human psyche and achieving psychological transformation. By engaging with these archetypes, individuals embark on a profound journey of self-awareness, ultimately facilitating the process of individuation and personal evolution. Furthermore, recognizing and working with these archetypal patterns enables individuals to tap into the collective unconscious, connecting with the shared symbolic reservoir of humanity.

4. Symbolism and Universal Patterns:

Symbolism, as manifested through archetypes, transcends cultural boundaries, offering a glimpse into the collective unconscious that dwells within each individual. These universal patterns are not confined by time or space; rather, they resonate across diverse cultures and epochs, reflecting fundamental aspects of human experience. From the primal motifs found in ancient cave paintings to the recurrent mythological narratives in various civilizations, the universal nature of symbolism reveals its enduring significance. Through this lens, we discern the recurring motifs of creation, transformation, death, rebirth, heroism, and the eternal struggle between opposing forces. The archetypal symbols encapsulate these timeless themes, mirroring the underlying structures that shape human consciousness. Their ubiquitous presence in art, literature, religion, and dreams attests to their pervasive influence on human thought and behavior. Moreover, the study of symbolism and universal patterns underscores the inherent interconnectedness of cultures and individuals, fostering a deeper appreciation for the shared human condition. It invites us to recognize the threads that unite us and to appreciate the diversity of expressions through which these archetypal symbols manifest. Embracing the symbolism and universal patterns embedded within the archetypes enriches our understanding of the human journey, instilling a sense of commonality that transcends cultural and societal divisions. Ultimately, the recognition of these universal patterns offers an opportunity for personal and collective growth, serving as a bridge between the individual and the collective unconscious.

5. Cultural and Psychological Relevance:

Archetypes, as universal symbols, hold profound implications on both individual and collective levels. In cultural contexts, archetypes manifest in myths, folklore, religious narratives, and art, influencing the ethos and values of a society. These symbolic patterns provide a rich tapestry that enriches cultural identities and informs collective consciousness. Moreover, archetypes serve as fundamental elements in shaping the narrative of a culture, often reflecting the collective aspirations, fears, and struggles of a community.

From a psychological perspective, the study of archetypes offers insights into the deep-seated motivations and behaviors of individuals. They resonate across diverse cultures, illustrating common human experiences and emotions. Understanding the archetypal dimensions can guide individuals towards self-discovery and personal growth, fostering a sense of connection to their cultural inheritance while traversing the complexities of modern life. Moreover, archetypes contribute to the construction of personal identity and play a crucial role in the individuation process, leading to a more integrated and fulfilled existence. By exploring the cultural and psychological significance of archetypes, we delve into the interplay between the human mind, societal frameworks, and collective unconscious.

6. Archetypes in Personal Development:

Archetypes, as universal symbols embedded within the collective unconscious, play a profound role in personal development. Understanding and integrating archetypal energies can lead to profound psychological growth and self-awareness. In the sphere of personal development, individuals may find themselves resonating with particular archetypal patterns, which can provide valuable insights into their own psyche.

The process of individuation, as conceptualized by Carl Jung, revolves around the recognition and assimilation of these archetypal energies. By engaging with archetypes, individuals embark on a journey of self-discovery, gradually uncovering latent aspects of their personality and gaining a deeper understanding of their motivations and behaviors.

Archetypes serve as potent catalysts for inner transformation, highlighting both the light and shadow aspects of the human psyche. For example, recognizing the presence of the 'hero' archetype within oneself can inspire courage, resilience, and a willingness to overcome obstacles. Conversely, acknowledging the 'shadow' archetype can bring awareness to repressed or neglected aspects of one's personality, paving the way for healing and integration.

The symbolic nature of archetypes enables individuals to connect with timeless themes and narratives that resonate across cultures and societies. This provides a sense of belonging and continuity, aiding individuals in managing life transitions and challenges. By embracing archetypal symbolism, individuals can enrich their inner world, accessing a wellspring of creativity, inspiration, and emotional depth.

Archetypes in personal development encompass not only the individual's internal landscape but also their interactions within the external world. Recognizing archetypal dynamics in relationships and social structures can foster empathy, compassion, and a broader appreciation of diverse perspectives. By recognizing archetypal patterns in others, individuals can cultivate a deeper understanding of human behavior and foster harmonious connections.

7. Transformative Power of Archetypal Symbols:

Archetypal symbols possess a transformative power that permeates various aspects of human experience. These universal symbols, deeply embedded in the collective unconscious, have been recognized for their capacity to catalyze personal growth, instigate profound shifts in perspective, and evoke profound emotional responses. The transformative power of archetypal symbols is rooted in their ability to resonate with fundamental human experiences and emotions across cultures and epochs. Through their resonance, these symbols serve as potent catalysts for self-discovery and psychological integration.

Archetypal symbols operate as conduits for the exploration of the subconscious mind, enabling individuals to confront and assimilate latent aspects of their psyche. This process of engagement with archetypal symbols often leads to profound transformations, as individuals gain insight into their innermost motivations, fears, and aspirations. Moreover, the transformative power inherent in archetypes extends beyond individual development, influencing societal dynamics, cultural narratives, and artistic expressions.

The transformative influence of archetypal symbols is linked to their role in facilitating the individuation process, as postulated by Jungian psychology. By engaging with archetypes, individuals embark on a journey toward self-realization, exploring the depths of their psyche and striving towards psychic wholeness. Uniting disparate aspects of the self, archetypal symbols foster internal harmony and integration, leading to an enriched sense of identity and purpose. Such transformation often unfolds through the reinterpretation and reintegration of archetypal symbolism within the context of personal narratives, thereby enhancing self-awareness and fostering holistic development.

Additionally, the transformative power of archetypal symbols is evident in various disciplines, including literature, art, and mythology, where these symbolic motifs serve as vehicles for transcending individual experiences and resonating with universal themes. Through the recognition and interpretation of these symbols, individuals are invited to explore the depth of human experience, elicit emotional catharsis, and transcend temporal and cultural boundaries. Ultimately, the transformative potential of archetypal symbols transcends their mere aesthetic or ideological significance, offering opportunities for personal and collective evolution.

8. Contemporary Interpretations of Archetypes:

In today's psychological landscape, numerous scholars and practitioners have contributed to the understanding of archetypes, offering diverse perspectives and applications. One prevalent contemporary interpretation is the integration of archetypal theory with modern neuroscience, which aims to explore the neurological foundations of universal symbols and their significance in shaping human cognition and behavior. By examining the neural correlates of archetypal patterns, researchers seek to elucidate how these primordial images and motifs manifest in the brain, thereby deepening our comprehension of the human psyche. Moreover, contemporary interpretations often emphasize the intersection of archetypes with cultural and social dimensions. This approach acknowledges that archetypes are not isolated entities but are dynamically influenced by the collective experiences and narratives of a society. As such, contemporary scholars delve into the interplay between archetypes and cultural dynamics, recognizing the role of societal constructs in shaping and modifying these universal symbols. Additionally, the advent of depth psychology and its integration with various therapeutic modalities has propelled contemporary interpretations of archetypes in clinical settings. Therapists now utilize archetypal imagery and symbolism as tools for accessing and addressing the unconscious aspects of the psyche, promoting healing and self-discovery. Furthermore, the application of archetypal frameworks in fields outside traditional psychology, such as literature, film, and marketing, has expanded the discourse on archetypes beyond academic circles. Contemporary interpretations recognize the pervasive influence of archetypes in shaping narratives, branding, and consumer behavior, unveiling the broad-reaching implications of these universal symbols. Moreover, interdisciplinary collaborations have enriched the contemporary understanding of archetypes, with contributions from fields such as anthropology, mythology, and philosophy. These diverse perspectives offer a holistic view of archetypes, demonstrating their relevance across different disciplines and fostering a more comprehensive comprehension of their role in human experience.

9. Critiques and Alternative Views on Archetypal Theory:

One prominent critique challenges the universal applicability of archetypes across different cultures and societies, emphasizing the potential for culturally specific symbols and narratives to shape individual and collective unconscious experiences. This perspective underscores the importance of considering socio-cultural influences in understanding the diversity of symbolic representations and meanings. Moreover, critics argue that the archetypal theory's deterministic nature may overlook the nuanced intricacies of personal experiences and the dynamic interplay between conscious and unconscious processes. By focusing on the rigidity of archetypal patterns, this critique raises meaningful questions about the adaptability and fluidity of symbolic interpretations in diverse psychological contexts.

In addition to critiques, alternative views on archetypal theory offer innovative frameworks that complement or challenge traditional Jungian perspectives. Some scholars propose a more interdisciplinary approach, integrating insights from neuroscience, cognitive psychology, and semiotics to enrich the understanding of archetypal phenomena. By examining the neurological correlates of symbolic processing and the cognitive mechanisms underlying archetypal imagery, these alternative views contribute to a multifaceted exploration of how archetypes manifest and operate within human consciousness. Furthermore, critical engagements with archetypal theory encourage a reevaluation of its categorical boundaries, opening avenues for hybrid models that blend Jungian concepts with contemporary developments in psychoanalysis and cultural studies.

The debate surrounding archetypal theory also encompasses discussions on the ethical implications of interpreting and applying universal symbols in therapeutic and educational settings. Ethicists and practitioners scrutinize the power dynamics embedded within the archetypal discourse, cautioning against essentializing or imposing symbolic frameworks onto individuals without acknowledging their agency and subjective interpretations. As such, an ethical inquiry into the responsible use of archetypal imagery and narratives urges professionals to manage the complexities of symbolic interventions with sensitivity to diverse cultural, social, and personal backgrounds.

## The Collective Unconscious - Depths of the Psyche

1. Introduction:

The concept of the collective unconscious represents a central pillar in the edifice of analytical psychology. Rooted in the rich tapestry of human history and cross-cultural mythology, the collective unconscious is a reservoir of primordial images and archetypes that transcend individual experiences and form the substratum of the human psyche. Jung's explication of the collective unconscious diverged from the prevalent theories of his time, drawing inspiration from diverse sources such as ancient mythologies, religious symbolism, dreams, and cross-cultural psychological studies. This innovative perspective challenged the predominant emphasis on conscious thought and behavior, elevating the unconscious to a paramount position in the understanding of human nature and behavior. The theoretical foundations of the collective unconscious underscore its synchronistic nature, where seemingly unrelated events and symbols are connected by underlying archetypal patterns that operate beyond the purview of individual consciousness. Thus, the collective unconscious is inherited and shared by all human beings, manifesting through universal themes and motifs across distinct cultures and historical periods.

2. Historical Context and Theoretical Foundations:

The concept of the collective unconscious originates from Jung's divergence from Freudian psychoanalysis, where he sought to elucidate the greater depths of the human mind beyond personal experiences and individual consciousness. Jung drew inspiration from diverse sources such as mythology, religion, philosophy, and anthropology to formulate his theory of the collective unconscious. His studies of various cultures and symbolic systems led him to propose the existence of universally inherited symbolic archetypes that shape human thought, emotions, and behaviors. This departure from the prevailing focus on conscious, rational processes marked a significant paradigm shift in psychological discourse.

The philosophical underpinnings directly influenced Jung's conceptualization of the collective unconscious. Integrating elements of metaphysical and spiritual dimensions, Jung's theory transcended conventional empirical approaches and ventured into the spheres of the ineffable and transcendent aspects of human experience. Furthermore, the theoretical foundations of the collective unconscious also reflect Jung's emphasis on individuation, a process through which an individual achieves self-realization and wholeness by integrating and reconciling disparate aspects of the psyche.

3. Constituents of the Collective Unconscious:

Defined by Carl Jung as the part of the unconscious mind that is derived from ancestral memory and experience, these constituents represent a universal reservoir of human knowledge and experience. It comprises archetypes, collectively inherited patterns of human behavior and thought, which form the basis of our perceptions, beliefs, and actions. The archetypes serve as symbolic representations of instinctual functioning and play a significant role in shaping our emotions, behaviors, and interactions.

The constituents of the collective unconscious encompass a wide array of archetypal symbols that reflect common themes found across diverse cultures and societies. These symbols, such as the hero, the mother, the shadow, and the wise old man, embody shared human experiences and provide a framework for understanding the universal aspects of human existence. They act as psychic blueprints, influencing our thoughts, feelings, and behaviors in ways that are often beyond conscious awareness.

The constituents of the collective unconscious operate within an individual's psyche, exerting a profound influence on personal development and psychological dynamics. Each person's unique combination of archetypes creates a distinctive psychological landscape that influences their perceptions, motivations, and relationships. By recognizing and understanding these constituents, individuals can gain insight into the underlying forces shaping their lives and explore the interconnectedness between their personal experiences and broader cultural and historical narratives.

In delving into the constituents of the collective unconscious, it becomes evident that they are not static or fixed entities but rather dynamic and evolving elements of the human psyche. Their manifestations can vary widely depending on an individual's cultural background, personal experiences, and developmental stage. Additionally, the interplay between these constituents and external factors, such as societal norms, family dynamics, and life events, further enriches their complexity and contribution to an individual's psychological makeup.

4. Archetypal Patterns and Their Influence:

Archetypal patterns represent universally recognized symbols and themes that have existed across cultures and civilizations throughout human history. These archetypes, as conceptualized by Jung, hold immense influence over individual psyches and societal dynamics, shaping our perceptions, behaviors, and cultural narratives.

The influence of archetypal patterns can be observed in various aspects of human experience, ranging from mythological narratives and religious symbolism to artistic expressions and dreams. For instance, the archetypal figure of the Hero appears in countless myths and legends, embodying the universal concept of courage, sacrifice, and triumph over adversity. Similarly, the archetype of the Mother symbolizes nurturing, protection, and fertility, recurring in diverse cultural contexts as a representation of the feminine nurturing principle.

These archetypal patterns exert their influence on individuals through the process of individuation, wherein the psyche assimilates and integrates these universal symbols into personal experiences and expressions. At the same time, they also shape collective attitudes, values, and institutions, serving as foundational elements that underpin societal structures and belief systems.

The influence of archetypal patterns extends beyond the field of psychology and culture, permeating fields such as literature, art, and religion. Many literary works and artistic creations incorporate archetypal motifs to evoke deep-seated emotions and resonate with universal human experiences. In religious contexts, archetypal figures often form the basis of spiritual narratives and rituals, providing individuals with a framework for understanding existential questions and finding meaning in life.

5. Personal vs. Collective Unconscious:

When considering the personal psyche, one encounters a wealth of unique experiences, memories, and traumas that shape an individual's worldview and behavioral patterns. This domain encompasses the specific, idiosyncratic elements that differentiate one person from another. In stark contrast, the collective unconscious underpins the shared reservoir of primordial images and archetypal motifs that transcend cultural and temporal boundaries, highlighting the interconnectedness of human consciousness.

Diving deeper into this comparative analysis unveils the distinctive characteristics of the personal and collective unconscious. The personal unconscious is primarily shaped by an individual's life experiences and comprises repressed emotions, forgotten memories, and internal conflicts. These elements form the basis of personal complexes and contribute to the diverse psychological makeup of each person. Conversely, the collective unconscious encapsulates universal themes and symbols that resonate across cultures and civilizations, such as the archetypes of the hero, the mother, and the shadow. These archetypal patterns are inherent in all human beings, acting as fundamental building blocks of the human psyche.

The manifestations of the personal and collective unconscious differ in their impact on cognition, behavior, and creativity. While the personal unconscious often influences immediate thoughts, feelings, and actions through individual experiences, the collective unconscious operates on a broader, more profound level. It exerts its influence through recurring symbols and mythological motifs that permeate art, literature, and religious traditions worldwide, transcending the boundaries of particular societies and histories.

6. Mechanisms of Influence:

The manifestations of the unconscious are characterized by their elusive and subtle nature, often surfacing in symbolic forms that require interpretation and analysis. These mechanisms of influence provide insight into the profound impact of the unconscious on human behavior, emotions, and cognition. One such mechanism is the phenomenon of dreams, which serves as a bridge between the conscious and unconscious spheres. Dreams are repositories of symbolic content that offer access to the unconscious processes, serving as a window into the deeper layers of the psyche. Another influential mechanism is the manifestation of archetypal imagery in cultural narratives, myths, and religious symbols. These archetypal motifs permeate human societies, shaping collective beliefs, values, and behaviors through their symbolic resonance. Moreover, the unconscious manifests through spontaneous creative expressions, such as art, literature, and rituals. These creative endeavors often serve as direct channels for the unconscious to express itself, providing a rich tapestry of symbolic representations. Furthermore, the unconscious exerts its influence through emotional and affective experiences, influencing interpersonal dynamics, intrapersonal conflicts, and behavioral patterns. The connections between the unconscious and these emotional manifestations underscore the pervasive power of unconscious forces. Additionally, the unconscious manifests through somatic experiences and bodily sensations, reflecting the interplay between psychological states and physical manifestations. These somatic expressions can unveil repressed emotions, unresolved conflicts, and psychosomatic dynamics. Finally, the unconscious also manifests through synchronistic events, inexplicable coincidences that hint at a deeper underlying order. These meaningful coincidences point towards the interconnectedness of the internal and external realities, offering glimpses of the unconscious orchestrating seemingly random occurrences.

7. Psychoanalytical Techniques:

Psychoanalytical techniques, rooted in the foundational principles of psychoanalysis, aim to uncover the hidden facets of the psyche and unravel the complex tapestry of the unconscious mind.

One prominent technique utilized in delving into the collective unconscious is free association. Through this method, individuals are encouraged to verbalize their thoughts without censorship, allowing for the spontaneous emergence of repressed emotions, memories, and symbols from the depths of the unconscious. By examining the patterns and underlying themes within these associations, psychoanalysts can discern the presence of archetypal elements and gain insight into the individual's deeper psychological landscape.

Another significant approach is dream analysis. Dreams act as a portal to the unconscious, offering a rich reservoir of symbolic content that reflects an individual's innermost concerns, conflicts, and aspirations. By interpreting the latent content of dreams—uncovering the symbolic representations woven within the narrative—psychoanalysts can decipher the messages communicated by the unconscious and shed light on the archetypal motifs that permeate the dreamer's psychological domain.

The use of active imagination, a method championed by Carl Jung, facilitates direct engagement with the contents of the unconscious. Through active imagination, individuals immerse themselves in a process of spontaneous visualization and inner dialogue, consciously interacting with the symbolic figures and scenarios that arise from the depths of the psyche. This technique offers a profound means of connecting with archetypal energies and integrating the fragmented aspects of the self, fostering a harmonious relationship between conscious awareness and the collective unconscious.

In addition to these methods, psychoanalytical techniques encompass the exploration of transference and countertransference dynamics, amplification of symbolic material, and the utilization of interpretative frameworks such as mythological parallels and cultural symbolism. The multifaceted nature of these techniques underscores the complexity of probing the collective unconscious and underscores the nuanced interplay between the individual and the archetypal forces that shape their psychic reality.

8. Relationship with Other Components of Psychodynamics:

Understanding how the collective unconscious interacts with other elements can provide valuable insights into the complex workings of the human psyche. At the core of psychodynamics lies the interplay between conscious and unconscious mental processes. The collective unconscious, distinct from the personal unconscious, is an essential component that underscores the universality of certain psychological phenomena. It intertwines with the personal unconscious, influencing individual experiences in subtle yet powerful ways. This relationship forms the foundation for understanding the dynamics of human behavior and personality.

In exploring the relationship between the collective unconscious and psychodynamics, it becomes evident that archetypal patterns, deeply ingrained in the collective unconscious, have a significant impact on emotional and behavioral manifestations. These archetypes, such as the anima/animus or the shadow, interact with conscious thoughts, desires, and actions, shaping an individual's experiences and perceptions. This interaction highlights the connections between the collective unconscious and conscious awareness, showcasing the fundamental role of archetypes in psychodynamic processes.

The collective unconscious influences interpersonal dynamics and societal structures, contributing to the formation of cultural norms, values, and symbols. Within the framework of psychodynamics, the collective unconscious serves as a reservoir of shared symbolic representations that underpin human interactions and relationships. By recognizing the influence of collective unconscious contents on interpersonal dynamics, one gains a deeper understanding of the underlying motivations and conflicts that shape social behavior and group dynamics.

When considering the relationship with other components of psychodynamics, it is essential to examine the implications for therapeutic practice. Psychodynamic approaches often involve delving into the depths of the unconscious mind to address unresolved conflicts and promote healing. The incorporation of collective unconscious dynamics in therapeutic interventions provides a comprehensive understanding of the underlying factors contributing to an individual's psychological well-being. By integrating the exploration of archetypal motifs and collective unconscious imagery into therapy, practitioners can facilitate profound transformations and foster holistic psychological development.

This interconnectedness also extends to the broader field of psychology, where the integration of the collective unconscious enriches our comprehension of human development, psychopathology, and psychotherapeutic modalities. By acknowledging the relationship between the collective unconscious and psychodynamics, psychologists and mental health professionals can refine their theoretical frameworks and clinical practices, thereby enhancing the effectiveness of therapeutic interventions and promoting psychological flourishing.

## The Self - The Center of Conscious Awareness

1. Introduction to the Concept of the Self:

in Jungian psychology, the concept of the self represents the center of conscious awareness and an essential element in the process of individuation. To comprehend the historical development of the self in Jungian psychology, it is imperative to delve into its foundational theories and definitions. Carl Jung, a pioneer in the field of analytical psychology, introduced the notion of the self as the archetype of wholeness and the center of the collective unconscious. According to Jung, the self represents the unification of all aspects of an individual's psyche, encompassing both the conscious and unconscious elements. This concept acknowledges the holistic nature of human consciousness and serves as a guiding principle in understanding the complex dynamics of the human mind. Another influential figure in the historical development of the self in Jungian psychology is Jung's exploration of Eastern philosophies and religious traditions. Jung's exposure to these cultural perspectives significantly influenced his conceptualization of the self, leading to a broader understanding of the universal and transcultural aspects of the self. Moreover, the rich tapestry of myths and symbols from various cultures further enriched Jung's understanding of the self as a universal symbol of unity. The archetypal nature of the self reflects its timeless and cross-cultural relevance, emphasizing its significance beyond individual experiences. The evolution of the self within Jungian psychology also encompasses the differentiation between the ego and the self. This differentiation forms the basis for comprehending the dynamic interplay between the conscious sense of self and the deeper, unconscious layers of the psyche. Jung's elucidation of this relationship underscores the pivotal role of the self in orchestrating the integration of disparate psychic elements, leading to personal wholeness and individuation. Furthermore, Jung's emphasis on the process of individuation as a transformative journey towards self-realization sheds light on the profound implications of the self in shaping the human experience.

2. Historical Development:

At the core of Jung's early conceptualization of the self was his divergence from Freudian psychoanalysis and the subsequent formation of analytical psychology. The notion of the self emerged gradually as Jung delved into the exploration of the unconscious and collective unconscious, drawing inspiration from diverse philosophical, religious, and mythological sources. This integration of varied influences underpinned the vast reservoir from which Jung derived the foundational elements of the self. The historical development of the self also reflects the journey of individuation, which Jung considered essential for achieving psychological wholeness. The process of individuation, interconnected with the evolution of the self, illustrates the path towards self-realization and integration of the conscious and unconscious aspects of the psyche. Moreover, the significance of symbols and archetypes in the historical narrative of the self cannot be understated. These universal and timeless motifs, as proposed by Jung, have dynamically shaped the construction and interpretation of the self, illustrating how historical developments have embraced and woven these symbolic elements into the fabric of Jungian psychology. Furthermore, the historical trajectory of the self within Jungian psychology illuminates the dynamism inherent in its definition and functionality, underscoring how the concept adapts and resonates with the experiences and contexts of individuals across diverse cultures and eras.

3. The Relationship between Ego and Self:

The ego, synonymous with one's conscious identity and rational perceptions, often functions as a window through which individuals engage with the external world. Conversely, the self represents the totality of the psyche, encompassing not only the conscious mind but also the unconscious layers, including archetypes and collective experiences.

Jung maintained that a harmonious relationship between the ego and the self is essential for psychological equilibrium and individuation – the process of becoming a unified and whole individual. This integration requires a confluence of the conscious and unconscious dimensions, leading to a balanced and authentic self-awareness. Nevertheless, achieving this alignment is not devoid of challenges; the ego often exhibits resistance to acknowledging and integrating elements of the self that lie beyond conscious awareness.

The ego's inclination to identify solely with conscious perceptions and rationality can lead to a dissociation from the deeper layers of the psyche, resulting in a fragmented sense of self. Consequently, individuals may experience inner conflicts, feelings of disconnection, or a sense of spiritual emptiness, signifying a lack of integration between the ego and the self.

In the context of therapeutic practice, Jungian analysts facilitate the exploration of the relationship between the ego and the self by delving into the conscious and unconscious manifestations of the psyche. Through techniques such as dream analysis, active imagination, and exploration of archetypal symbols, individuals are encouraged to recognize and integrate aspects of the self that have been neglected or suppressed by the ego's dominance.

Individuals are guided in understanding the influences of cultural, societal, and familial conditioning on the development of the ego-self relationship. The impact of external factors on shaping an individual's egoic identity and its interaction with the deeper layers of the self is integral to fostering a comprehensive awareness of the psyche.

4. Conscious Awareness - Perceptions and Realities:

Conscious awareness encompasses the perception and interpretation of reality. In the context of Jungian psychology, it plays a pivotal role in the individuation process, where individuals strive to integrate the various aspects of their psyche into a harmonious whole. Perceptions, shaped by personal experiences, cultural influences, and archetypal patterns, significantly impact one's conscious awareness. These perceptions can often lead to subjective realities that influence an individual's understanding of the world and themselves. The interplay between conscious awareness, perceptions, and realities is complex and multifaceted. Jungian theory emphasizes the examination of how an individual's conscious awareness is influenced by their internal and external environments. It prompts a deep exploration of how perceptions are formed and the transformative power of shifting these perceptions. Furthermore, it delves into the significance of reconciling inner conflicts and integrating unconscious content into conscious awareness. Understanding the nuances of conscious awareness involves exploration of the unconscious biases, societal conditioning, and individual psychological predispositions that shape one's perception of reality. This self-reflective process requires a willingness to confront the shadow aspects of the self and examine the authenticity of one's conscious awareness. Moreover, it demands the recognition of projection and its impact on perceiving external stimuli, leading to distortions in conscious awareness. The richness of consciousness and the diversity of human experiences contribute to the vast tapestry of perceptions and realities. Acknowledging this diversity is crucial for expanding one's conscious awareness and developing empathy and understanding toward others' subjective realities. Importantly, Jungian psychology emphasizes the transcendence of limited perspectives and the ability to embrace the paradoxes inherent in conscious awareness. The journey toward a more expansive and inclusive conscious awareness involves engaging with symbols, dreams, and creative expressions as tools for unlocking deeper layers of the psyche. Ultimately, cultivating a heightened conscious awareness fosters a greater sense of connection with the self, others, and the world at large.

5. The Self as an Integrative Agent:

At the heart of Jungian psychology lies the concept of the self as an integrative agent, acting as a unifying force within the psyche. The self serves as a center of organization, harmonizing disparate elements of an individual's personality. It encompasses the conscious and unconscious aspects, bringing together the various archetypal influences and integrating them into a coherent whole. Through this integration, the self facilitates the process of individuation, guiding individuals towards self-realization and psychological wholeness.

Central to the notion of the self as an integrative agent is the idea that it acts as a mediator between the conscious ego and the deep layers of the unconscious, particularly the collective unconscious. By serving as a bridge between these dimensions, the self enables a dialogue between the conscious mind and the archetypal forces that shape human experience. This interplay between the self and the broader unconscious landscape underscores the significance of the self in reconciling conflicts and fostering inner harmony.

The self operates as a stabilizing force amidst the dynamic interplay of archetypes within the psyche. It tempers the erratic tendencies of the unconscious, providing a sense of cohesion and stability to an individual's psychological landscape. In doing so, the self aids in the management of psychic energy, ensuring that it is directed towards constructive personal development rather than chaotic dispersion.

The integrative function of the self is exemplified in the process of dream analysis, a cornerstone of Jungian therapy. Dreams often express the tensions and conflicts within an individual's psyche, and through the interpretive lens of Jungian psychology, it becomes evident that the self plays a pivotal role in synthesizing these diverse elements. As dreams unfold, the self emerges as a guiding force, weaving together the disparate symbols and themes into a meaningful narrative, thereby offering individuals insight into their inner workings.

The self's integrative capacity unfolds in the context of creative expression and artistic endeavors. Artists, in particular, often tap into the wellsprings of the unconscious, channeling archetypal energies into their creations. Here, the self acts as a facilitator, allowing for the transformation of raw unconscious material into coherent and meaningful artistic expressions. Thus, the self not only unifies the individual psyche but also mediates the externalization of profound unconscious contents.

6. Self vs. the Collective Unconscious:

While the collective unconscious represents the repository of universal symbols and archetypes shared by all individuals, the self encapsulates the center of conscious awareness within an individual's psyche. This distinction forms the cornerstone of individuation, allowing for the integration and harmonization of various psychic elements. The self, as posited by Jung, operates as an organizing principle that strives for wholeness and balance, while the collective unconscious serves as the reservoir of primordial images and instinctual patterns common to humanity. Understanding this demarcation is pivotal for comprehending the dynamics of the human mind and the journey towards self-realization.

In essence, the self embodies the individuated and unique aspects of an individual's personality, encompassing their conscious experiences, perceptions, and identity. It relates to the sphere of ego consciousness, where personal choices, beliefs, and values are shaped. On the other hand, the collective unconscious transcends personal narratives, delving into the deeper layers of the psyche, housing archetypal structures and mythic motifs that influence human behavior and cultural manifestations across time and space. These archetypes, such as the shadow, anima/animus, and the wise old man, are ingrained in the collective unconscious, exerting profound influences on individual lives.

The differentiation between the self and the collective unconscious elucidates the interplay between the conscious and unconscious dimensions of the psyche. While the self primarily pertains to conscious awareness, the collective unconscious operates beyond immediate awareness, exerting its influence through dreams, fantasies, and creative expressions. Recognizing and discerning the manifestations of the collective unconscious from the individual self is crucial for achieving psychological equilibrium and fostering personal growth. Through this process, individuals can acknowledge and integrate unconscious contents, thereby achieving a deeper understanding of themselves and their place within the broader human experience.

The delineation between the self and the collective unconscious underscores the significance of self-awareness and introspection in traversing the complexities of one's inner world. This involves acknowledging and reconciling with the shadow aspects, embracing the anima/animus dynamics, and embodying the wisdom inherent in the collective unconscious. Ultimately, this differentiation fosters a profound sense of personal empowerment and purpose.

7. The Process of Self-Realization:

Self-realization involves the conscious recognition and integration of one's true identity and potential. This process encompasses a profound journey of self-discovery and awareness, where individuals strive to uncover their authentic selves amid the complexities of societal influences, cultural norms, and personal experiences. Self-realization in Jungian psychology is not merely a cognitive realization but a holistic transformation that encompasses the emotional, spiritual, and psychological dimensions of an individual's being.

The process of self-realization often begins with a period of introspection and reflection, where individuals examine their beliefs, values, and life experiences in an attempt to gain deeper insight into themselves. This introspective phase may involve exploring one's strengths, weaknesses, aspirations, and underlying motivations, leading to a heightened sense of self-awareness and clarity about one's purpose and direction in life. It also entails confronting and transcending the various archetypal influences and unconscious patterns that may hinder the authentic expression of the self.

Self-realization comprises a dynamic interplay between the personal and collective unconscious, as individuals move through the web of archetypal energies that shape their psyche. Jung emphasized the significance of engaging with the unconscious through dreams, active imagination, and symbolic exploration as integral components of the self-realization process. By elucidating the symbolic manifestations and messages inherent in the unconscious, individuals can embark on a transformative journey towards embracing a more integrated and balanced sense of self.

The process of self-realization involves the recognition and integration of the shadow—a complex aspect of the psyche containing repressed or disowned elements of the self. Through courageous exploration and acknowledgment of the shadow, individuals can embrace their hidden potentials and reconcile inner conflicts, ultimately fostering a greater sense of wholeness and authenticity.

Additionally, the journey of self-realization often unfolds within the context of relationships, social interactions, and cultural dynamics. Individuals may encounter various challenges and opportunities for growth as they move through the evolving landscapes of personal and interpersonal connections. Furthermore, the pursuit of self-realization extends beyond individual introspection and encompasses the broader societal implications of identity, empowerment, and collective transformation.

In conclusion, the process of self-realization is a multifaceted and transformative odyssey that calls upon individuals to embark on a profound inward quest toward discovering and integrating their true selves. It encompasses the unearthing of one's inherent potentials, the reconciliation of conflicting aspects of the psyche, and the forging of an authentic and empowered identity. Ultimately, self-realization serves as a catalyst for personal growth, liberation, and the realization of one's highest aspirations.

8. Challenges in Understanding the Self Across Cultures:

Understanding the self is a complex endeavor, and when viewed through the lens of culture, this complexity is further amplified.

Cultural diversity significantly impacts how individuals perceive and construct their sense of self. Cultural norms and values play a pivotal role in shaping individuals' identities and their interpretations of the self. For instance, individualistic cultures emphasize personal achievement and independence, fostering a self-concept centered on autonomy and distinctiveness. In contrast, collectivist cultures prioritize group harmony and interdependence, leading to a more interconnected and relationally oriented sense of self. These fundamental differences necessitate a nuanced understanding of the diverse self-concepts that emerge within different cultural frameworks.

Language barriers also contribute to the intricacy of deciphering the self across cultures. The linguistic nuances and subtleties of self-expression vary across languages, impacting how individuals articulate and comprehend their inner experiences. Moreover, certain cultures may lack direct translations for concepts related to the self, posing challenges in accurately capturing the depth of self-awareness and identity exploration.

Religious and spiritual beliefs further shape the understanding of the self within cultural paradigms. Divergent belief systems offer contrasting perspectives on the nature of the self, its purpose, and its connection to the transcendent. These variations not only influence individual self-perceptions but also impact communal understandings of identity, morality, and existential meaning.

Social roles and expectations within different cultures also pose significant challenges in understanding the self. Gender roles, familial dynamics, and societal hierarchies all influence how individuals perceive themselves and construct their identities within specific cultural contexts. Furthermore, the evolving nature of globalization and intercultural interaction introduces further complexities, as individuals engage with multiple cultural influences, leading to hybridized self-concepts that transcend traditional cultural boundaries.

Ultimately, managing the challenges of understanding the self across cultures requires a heightened sensitivity to cultural diversity and an openness to embracing the richness of varied perspectives. It calls for cultivating cultural competence, engaging in cross-cultural dialogue, and acknowledging the fluidity of identity within an increasingly interconnected world.

9. The Significance of the Self in Personal Growth:

The exploration of the self across cultures has revealed the profound significance of individual consciousness in personal growth and development. Across diverse cultural contexts, the journey towards self-realization remains a universal aspiration, yet the paths to achieving this goal may vary considerably. Despite these variations, one common thread emerges—the inherent need for individuals to gain a deeper understanding of themselves. This process of introspection and self-discovery is paramount in fostering personal growth and wellbeing.

When individuals embark on the quest for self-discovery, they often encounter internal conflicts and obstacles that challenge their established beliefs and perceptions. The confrontations with the shadow aspects of the self, as proposed by Jungian psychology, can be particularly transformative, requiring individuals to grapple with their hidden motives and suppressed emotions. Through this introspective process, individuals can attain heightened self-awareness, leading to an alignment with their authentic selves. As a result, they are better equipped to manage life's complexities and to foster meaningful relationships with others.

The significance of the self in personal growth extends beyond individual well-being and permeates various spheres of human existence. From a societal standpoint, individuals who have undergone significant self-realization are more likely to exhibit social responsibility and empathy towards others. By cultivating a deep understanding of their own psyche, such individuals can break free from the constraints of societal conditioning and contribute positively to their communities. When many individuals collectively strive towards self-realization, the resultant social fabric becomes enriched with compassion, harmony, and tolerance. Through this collective elevation of consciousness, societal conflicts based on ignorance and prejudice are diminished, thus contributing to the greater good of humanity.

In conclusion, the concept of the self serves as the foundation upon which individuals build their understanding of the world and their place within it. Regardless of cultural differences, the journey towards self-realization is a fundamental human experience, shaping not only individual lives but also the dynamics of broader society.

## Relations Between Archetypes and the Collective Unconscious

1. Introduction to Archetypal Dynamics:

Archetypes serve as innate psychic structures, shaping our perceptions, behaviors, and experiences. They form the primordial essence of human existence, embodying timeless patterns of human thought and emotion. Understanding archetypal dynamics necessitates an in-depth examination of the collective unconscious, a reservoir of inherited psychic material shared by all individuals irrespective of culture or upbringing. Here, the archetypes reside as autonomous and numinous entities, exerting profound influences on our conscious lives. By scrutinizing their manifestations, we get insights into the symbolic language through which the collective unconscious communicates. Moreover, this exploration paves the way for comprehending the universal themes and motifs that underpin human narratives and mythologies across diverse societies. A critical aspect of these dynamics lies in the individuation process, where individuals strive to integrate and reconcile the disparate archetypal forces within their psyche. This endeavor underscores the transformative potential of archetypes, as they propel individuals towards self-realization and wholeness. Additionally, the interconnectedness of archetypes and the collective unconscious unveils the profound relevance of these concepts in various domains, including literature, art, religion, and cultural practices.

2. The Collective Unconscious in Relation to Archetypes:

Rooted in the idea that all individuals share a common reservoir of inherited experiences and potentials, the collective unconscious serves as a repository for universal symbolic patterns and motifs, forming the basis for the manifestation of archetypes. These archetypes, deeply ingrained in the collective unconscious, exert a significant influence on an individual's thoughts, emotions, behaviors, and perceptions, often operating at an unconscious level.

In exploring the relationship between the collective unconscious and archetypes, it is essential to grasp the historical context and theoretical foundations that underpin Jungian psychology. Drawing from diverse cultural and mythological sources, Jung identified recurring motifs and symbols that transcend temporal and geographical boundaries, reflecting the presence of archetypes within the collective unconscious. These archetypal images are not static; rather, they evolve and adapt to the cultural milieu, shaping narratives and expressions that resonate across diverse populations.

The interconnectedness of Jungian constructs becomes evident when considering the symbiotic link between the collective unconscious and archetypes. The collective unconscious serves as the wellspring from which archetypes emerge, embodying fundamental organizing principles that govern human experiences and representations. As such, the manifestations of archetypes in dreams, fantasies, and cultural artifacts offer glimpses into the underlying dynamics of the collective unconscious, illuminating the profound impact of archetypal energies on individual and collective psyches.

The symbolic manifestations of archetypes within the collective unconscious hold immense psychological significance. These timeless, cross-cultural symbols encapsulate profound layers of meaning, evoking primordial emotions and insights that transcend rational comprehension. Through introspective exploration and therapeutic engagement, individuals can uncover and integrate these archetypal motifs, leading to enhanced self-awareness, personal growth, and individuation.

Beyond theoretical conjectures, empirical observations and case studies provide valuable insights into the practical implications of the collective unconscious and its relationship with archetypes. By examining the recurring themes and symbols that permeate individuals' dreams, artistic expressions, and cultural narratives, researchers and practitioners gain a deeper understanding of the archetypal dynamics at play within the collective unconscious. This empirical evidence lends credence to the enduring relevance of Jung's conceptualizations in understanding the human psyche across diverse contexts and populations.

Additionally, acknowledging the role of cultural influences on archetypal expressions unveils the dynamic interplay between the collective unconscious and sociocultural factors. As cultural myths, rituals, and traditions influence the salience and representation of archetypes, individuals' experiences and interpretations within specific cultural milieus contribute to the richness and diversity of archetypal manifestations within the collective unconscious. This cultural lens expands the discourse surrounding archetypal phenomena, emphasizing the need to contextualize their expressions within sociocultural frameworks.

Recognizing disruptions and blockages in archetypal interactions offers valuable insight into the complexities of the human psyche. Instances where individuals experience alienation or distortion of archetypal energies underscore the web of psychological forces at play within the collective unconscious. Exploring these disruptions catalyzes investigations into the sources of psychological distress and dissonance, warranting interventions aimed at restoring harmonious archetypal interactions and fostering psychological integration.

3. Interconnectedness of Jungian Constructs:

In delving into the intricacies of Jungian psychology, it becomes evident that the constructs within this theoretical framework are inherently interconnected, each influencing and shaping the others in a complex web of psychological phenomena. At the heart of this interconnectedness lies the concept of archetypes, which serve as fundamental psychic structures representing universal patterns and images. The collective unconscious, another pivotal construct, houses these archetypes and provides the psychic space for their expression and manifestation. It is through the interplay of these archetypal forces and the collective unconscious that the individual psyche is both influenced and shaped. Moreover, the concept of the Self, which stands as the center of conscious awareness, is deeply intertwined with these archetypal influences. Within the process of individuation, the Self seeks to integrate and harmonize the various archetypal energies, leading to a greater sense of wholeness and individuated identity. Notably, the dynamics of inner conflict, particularly the interplay between the ego and the Self, further underscore the interconnectedness within the Jungian framework. As the ego grapples with the demands of the Self and the manifestations of archetypal energies, the delicate balance of the psyche is continually negotiated and re-negotiated. This negotiation is often underscored by the symbolic manifestations of archetypes, which can emerge in dreams, myths, and cultural narratives. These symbolic expressions serve as profound indicators of the interconnectedness of archetypal forces within the human psyche, offering rich insights into the universal nature of these psychic structures. Additionally, the cultural implications of these archetypal manifestations cannot be overlooked, as cultural influences and collective symbols play a pivotal role in shaping individual psyches. Through the study of empirical observations and case studies, the nuanced interconnectedness of these Jungian constructs becomes even more palpable. These real-world instances offer valuable insights into how archetypal influences, interconnected with the collective unconscious and the individuation process, shape and mold individual experiences.

Furthermore, disruptions and blockages in archetypal interactions shed light on the intricacies and challenges inherent in traversing the interconnected terrain of the Jungian psyche.

4. Psychological Implications of Archetype Interaction:

The interplay of archetypes often manifests in various forms, such as dreams, fantasies, and interpersonal relationships. These manifestations provide valuable insights into an individual's inner world and can serve as significant indicators for psychological analysis and interpretation. Moreover, the identification and exploration of archetypal interactions can unveil hidden motivations, conflicts, and unresolved issues within the psyche, opening pathways for self-discovery and healing.

The psychological implications of archetype interaction extend beyond the individual level to encompass societal and cultural dimensions. The collective expressions of archetypes shape cultural myths, rituals, and ideologies, thereby influencing societal norms and values. Understanding how archetypes interact within the collective psyche of a culture can provide invaluable perspectives on collective behaviors, belief systems, and societal developments. Additionally, recognizing the archetypal underpinnings of cultural phenomena can shed light on social dynamics, historical trends, and facilitate cross-cultural understanding and dialogue.

Considering the psychological implications of archetype interaction also holds relevance in therapeutic practices and psychoanalytic approaches. By exploring and mapping out the dynamics of archetype interaction within a patient's psyche, therapists can gain deeper insights into the underlying causes of psychological distress, maladaptive patterns, and unresolved conflicts. This understanding paves the way for tailored interventions, aimed at promoting individuation and fostering psychological integration. Furthermore, acknowledging the web of archetypal interactions can guide individuals towards a more profound understanding of themselves, facilitating personal growth and wholeness.

5. Disruptions and Blockages in Archetypal Interactions:

The dynamics of archetypal interactions within the collective unconscious are integral to understanding the psyche's functioning. However, it is essential to explore the potential disruptions and blockages that can occur within this framework. Disruptions in archetypal interactions may manifest in various forms, such as archetypal conflicts, suppression, or distortion of archetypal energies. These disruptions can impede the individuation process and lead to psychological distress. Blockages in archetypal interactions may stem from unresolved psychic conflicts, trauma, or cultural impositions on personal archetypal manifestations. When these blockages persist, they can hinder a person's journey towards wholeness and self-realization. It is crucial to acknowledge that these disruptions and blockages are not uncommon and can significantly impact an individual's psychological well-being. Understanding the signs and symptoms of these disruptions is paramount for therapists and individuals alike. As the manifestations of these disruptions can be subtle or overt, a keen awareness of their potential effects on one's psychology is imperative. Addressing disruptions and blockages in archetypal interactions often requires a multi-faceted approach. Therapeutic interventions may involve exploring the origins of these disruptions through psychoanalytical techniques, dream analysis, and active imagination exercises. Moreover, integrating cultural perspectives can provide valuable insights into how societal influences contribute to disrupting archetypal interactions. By acknowledging and addressing disruptions and blockages within archetypal interactions, individuals can embark on a path towards resolving inner conflicts and achieving greater psychological integration. Furthermore, recognizing the impact of such disruptions also sheds light on the importance of cultural sensitivity in therapeutic practices. Cultural considerations play a significant role in discerning the manifestation and disruption of archetypal interactions, highlighting the need for a holistic approach to psychological healing.

## The Self and Its Integrative Function in Individuation

1. The Role of the Self in Psychological Integration:

The Self plays a pivotal role in psychological integration by serving as a guiding force that brings harmony to the various components of the psyche. It acts as a unifying principle, nurturing a sense of inner coherence and completeness. Through the process of individuation, individuals embark on a transformative journey towards self-realization, guided by the inherent wisdom of the Self. This process involves transcending the confines of the ego and integrating unconscious elements into conscious awareness, leading to a more balanced and authentic expression of one's identity.

A fundamental aspect of the Self's integrative function lies in its ability to foster alignment between conscious and unconscious processes. Jung emphasized the significance of integrating unconscious contents, such as archetypal imagery and symbolic representations, into conscious awareness. This alignment facilitates a deeper understanding of the dynamics at play within the psyche, enabling individuals to confront and reconcile conflicting elements. By engaging with the symbolic language of the unconscious, individuals gain insights into their profound inner workings, paving the way for psychological growth and transformation.

Symbolism and manifestations of the Self serve as potent expressions of its integrative function. The Self often emerges in dreams, myths, and religious symbols, embodying archetypal images that resonate across cultures and epochs. These manifestations provide individuals with profound symbolic representations of wholeness and offer glimpses into the transcendent dimensions of the psyche. Exploring these symbolic expressions fosters a deeper connection with the Self and encourages the integration of diverse psychic elements, contributing to psychological balance and fulfillment.

Distinguishing the Self from the ego is essential in understanding its role in psychological integration. While the ego represents the conscious aspect of the personality, shaped by social and cultural influences, the Self transcends these limitations, encompassing the entire range of psychic contents. Recognizing the distinction between the ego and the Self allows individuals to undertake the individuation process with clarity, acknowledging the transformative potential inherent in aligning with the wisdom of the Self.

2. Alignment Between Conscious and Unconscious Processes:

According to Jung, the unconscious exerts a powerful influence on conscious experience, shaping thoughts, emotions, and behaviors in ways that are often not immediately apparent. This hidden sphere of the psyche contains repressed memories, unresolved conflicts, and latent potentials, all of which can exert a profound impact on our conscious lives. As individuals progress through the process of individuation, they are tasked with bringing these unconscious elements into alignment with their conscious awareness. This integration marks a significant milestone in personal development, allowing for a more harmonious and balanced existence.

Achieving alignment between conscious and unconscious processes involves delving into the depths of the psyche, confronting the shadow aspects that have been relegated to the unconscious, and acknowledging their influence on conscious behavior. Through introspection, dream analysis, and active imagination, individuals can begin to bridge the gap between these two dimensions, fostering a deeper understanding of their inner world and its impact on external reality. By shining a light on the contents of the unconscious, individuals can transform disowned aspects of themselves into sources of strength and wisdom. This process not only leads to greater self-awareness but also empowers individuals to live authentically and make conscious choices that align with their true nature.

The alignment between conscious and unconscious processes enhances cognitive coherence and emotional regulation. By integrating unconscious contents, individuals gain a more comprehensive understanding of their motivations, fears, and desires, thereby facilitating a more holistic approach to decision-making and problem-solving. This heightened self-awareness mitigates internal conflicts and fosters emotional resilience, enabling individuals to manage life's challenges with greater equilibrium. Furthermore, the alignment of conscious and unconscious processes paves the way for creative expression, as it taps into the wellspring of symbolic imagery and archetypal themes that reside in the unconscious. This synthesis invigorates artistic endeavors, philosophical explorations, and spiritual pursuits, enriching the individual's experience of meaning and purpose.

3. Symbolism and Manifestations of the Self:

In Jungian psychology, the concept of the self is often symbolized in various forms across different cultures and historical contexts. The self's manifestations are diverse and can be found in religious symbols, mythological figures, dreams, and individual artistic expressions. These symbols serve as a bridge between the conscious ego and the unconscious, providing a means for the individuation process to unfold through symbolism.

One common manifestation of the self is the mandala, a circular symbol that represents the wholeness and unity of the self. The patterns and geometric designs within the mandala reflect the complexity and harmony of the psyche. Mandala creation, whether through art or meditation, has been proposed as a transformative tool for integrating unconscious elements with conscious awareness.

Another significant manifestation of the self is found in religious iconography, such as the concept of the higher self in Eastern philosophies or the image of Christ as a symbol of transcendence and spiritual unity in Christianity. These symbols provide individuals with representations that can guide them towards a deeper understanding of the self and its connection to the collective unconscious.

Dreams also serve as a rich source of symbolic manifestations of the self. Jung emphasized the importance of analyzing dream symbols to uncover unconscious aspects of the self. Symbolic images in dreams, such as a divine figure or a central guiding force, often represent the presence of the self and offer valuable insights into an individual's journey of self-realization.

Artistic expression, including literature, visual arts, and music, often serves as a vehicle through which the self's manifestations are conveyed. Through creativity, individuals can tap into the depths of the unconscious and bring forth symbolic representations of the self, thereby facilitating the integration of unconscious contents into conscious awareness.

4. The Journey of Self-Realization:

The journey of self-realization emphasizes the quest for integrating the fragmented aspects of the psyche to achieve personal wholeness. This transformative process involves delving deep into the inner dimensions of the unconscious, exploring the symbolic manifestations of the self, and understanding the dynamics of the individuation journey. As individuals embark on this profound odyssey, they encounter archetypal images and symbols that reflect the potential for growth and transformation within the psyche. These symbols serve as guideposts, illuminating the path towards self-realization and facilitating the integration of unconscious contents with conscious awareness. The journey of self-realization is not merely a linear progression but rather a cyclical and non-linear process, marked by periods of upheaval, crisis, and renewal. It demands an individual's willingness to confront their shadow aspects, embrace their personal myth, and manage the complexities of the collective unconscious. Moreover, self-realization involves recognizing the interconnectedness between the personal and collective psyche, acknowledging the archetypal patterns that underpin human experiences.

Throughout this transformative voyage, individuals are called to unearth the depths of their being, unraveling layers of conditioning, societal influences, and inherited narratives to reveal the authentic core of the self. The journey of self-realization often unfolds through various stages, encompassing self-reflection, introspection, and emotional catharsis. It necessitates a thorough exploration of one's beliefs, values, and aspirations, as well as an examination of the existential questions that pervade human existence. Furthermore, the process of self-realization invites individuals to cultivate a harmonious relationship between their conscious ego and the transcendent aspects of the self. By attuning to the inner stirrings of the psyche, individuals can gain profound insights into their innate potential and purpose, propelling them towards a more authentic and fulfilling way of being. Ultimately, the journey of self-realization culminates in the attainment of psychological wholeness, where individuals integrate the disparate aspects of the self, embrace their uniqueness, and embody a sense of completeness.

5. The Self vs. the Ego:

The differentiation between the self and the ego is a central concept in Jungian psychology. The ego represents our conscious identity, encompassing our thoughts, feelings, and personal experiences that we are aware of. It acts as the interface with the external world, enabling us to function in society and interact with others. On the other hand, the self, according to Jung, embodies the totality of the psyche, including both the conscious and unconscious aspects. It is the central archetype that serves as the blueprint for our potential wholeness and integration. Distinguishing between the self and the ego requires a deep exploration of the various layers of the psyche. The ego tends to operate within the sphere of individuality and personal identity, often driven by societal expectations and cultural conditioning. In contrast, the self transcends individual boundaries and connects us to the collective unconscious and universal archetypes. Understanding this distinction is essential for initiating the journey of self-realization and achieving psychological wholeness. The ego often seeks validation from external sources, striving for recognition and affirmation in the external world. In comparison, the self operates from a place of inner wisdom and authenticity, guiding us towards realizing our true potential and purpose. Recognizing the dynamics between the self and the ego enables individuals to manage the complexities of their inner worlds, fostering a harmonious relationship between the conscious and unconscious aspects of the psyche. Without acknowledging and integrating the self into our conscious awareness, individuals may experience feelings of emptiness, disconnection, and a lack of purpose. As one delves deeper into understanding the self and its distinctiveness from the ego, the process of individuation becomes more attainable, leading to a transformative journey of self-discovery and integration. Embracing the self involves confronting the shadow aspects of the psyche, embracing vulnerability, and reclaiming disowned elements of the self.

**Dynamics of Inner Conflict - Balance between Ego and Self:**

1. What is the Ego?

The ego serves as the conscious mind's center and is responsible for decision-making, rational thought processes, and one's sense of identity. It acts as a mediator between the individual's external environment and the innate drives emanating from the unconscious. In essence, the ego functions as a filter, processing and organizing perceptions to ensure adaptation and survival in the external world.

The ego is responsible for formulating a coherent narrative of an individual's experiences, thus contributing to the construction of personal identity. This narrative is deeply intertwined with the individual's sense of self and provides a framework through which they perceive and interpret the world. However, it is critical to note that the ego's perception of self may be influenced by cultural and societal factors, which can shape one's understanding of their identity and place in the world.

The ego operates based on the principle of reality, making decisions that align with the demands and norms of the external environment. It constantly seeks to maintain a balance between internal desires and external constraints, often managing the dynamics between personal needs and societal expectations. This negotiation between the individual and the external world lays the foundation for the development of one's personality and character.

Additionally, the ego exhibits distinct characteristics, including its ability to adapt to changing circumstances, process information through conscious reasoning, and maintain a coherent sense of self. It is also susceptible to the influences of the collective unconscious, wherein archetypal forces shape and influence its functions, often leading to conflicts and opportunities for growth.

2. Tensions Between Ego and Self:

The interplay between the ego and the self forms the crux of Jungian psychology. At the heart of this interplay lies the tension arising from the inherent opposites embodied by the ego and the self. The ego, representing our conscious identity and rational thought processes, constantly seeks to maintain control, security, and a sense of individuality. On the other hand, the self encompasses the entire psychic totality, inclusive of both conscious and unconscious elements, striving for wholeness and integration. This intrinsic duality gives rise to profound conflicts within the individual's psyche, manifesting as a struggle for dominance and equilibrium.

Central to the analysis of these tensions is the concept of individuation – the process of integrating disparate aspects of one's personality to achieve a unified whole. The ego, often driven by societal demands and external influences, maintains a defensive posture against the self's persistent call for authenticity and self-realization. This leads to a profound inner conflict, where the conscious mind's desire for stability and security clashes with the self's innate push for growth and transformation. Moreover, the ego's identification with social norms and constructs often opposes the self's inclination towards embracing the depth of the unconscious and acknowledging the shadow aspects of the psyche.

The tensions between the ego and the self are exacerbated by the dynamic nature of their relationship. As the self continually communicates its insights and messages through symbols, dreams, and intuitions, the ego is tasked with interpreting and incorporating these signals into conscious awareness. This process can lead to resistance and denial by the ego, fearing the dissolution of its established identity and cognitive frameworks. Consequently, the ego often engages in rationalization, projection, and other defense mechanisms to protect itself from the transformative demands of the self. However, such defensive maneuvers only serve to intensify the underlying tensions, hindering the individual's progress towards wholeness.

The resolution of these tensions requires a delicate and nuanced approach, involving the acknowledgment and acceptance of both egoic and self-oriented perspectives. This necessitates fostering a conscious dialogue between the ego and the self, facilitating an ongoing negotiation where each aspect contributes to the individual's psychological development.

3. Mechanisms of Psychological Defense:

Psychological defense mechanisms are crucial elements in understanding the dynamics of inner conflict as proposed by Jungian psychology. These mechanisms serve as adaptive strategies employed by the ego to protect itself against anxiety and maintain a semblance of psychological equilibrium. Understanding these defense mechanisms provides insight into how individuals cope with internal conflicts between the ego and the self. One of the primary defense mechanisms is repression, wherein thoughts, emotions, or impulses that are deemed unacceptable or threatening to the conscious mind are pushed into the unconscious. This process safeguards the ego from being overwhelmed by disturbing content and, consequently, maintains a sense of stability. Projection is another fundamental defense mechanism, where individuals attribute their own unwanted thoughts, feelings, or impulses onto others, thereby avoiding direct confrontation with their internal conflicts. Rationalization involves justifying one's actions or emotions in a manner that appears logical and socially acceptable, thus shielding the individual from discomfort associated with conflicting beliefs or desires. In the context of inner conflict, these defense mechanisms manifest as tools utilized by the ego to mitigate the unsettling impact of the self's demands for growth and integration. Furthermore, displacement serves as a pivotal defense mechanism, allowing the individual to redirect their emotional impulses from an original, possibly intimidating source, to a less confronting or safer target. This modulation aids in preventing potential destruction of the ego's established boundaries, enabling a semblance of stability to be maintained. As Jung himself emphasized, awareness of these mechanisms is crucial as it enables individuation – the process by which the individual seeks to achieve a harmonious relationship between the ego and the self. Acknowledging and engaging with these defense mechanisms forms an integral part of transcending inner conflicts and fostering holistic psychological development.

4. Role of Shadow in Inner Conflicts:

The concept of the shadow, as proposed by Carl Jung, represents the repressed or undeveloped aspects of an individual's personality that are often seen as negative, undesirable, or socially unacceptable. These aspects may include but are not limited to one's fears, insecurities, and unresolved traumas. In the context of inner conflicts, the shadow exerts a profound influence on an individual's thoughts, emotions, and behaviors. It is crucial to recognize that the shadow is not inherently malevolent; rather, it reflects the unacknowledged components of the psyche.

When left unrecognized or unaddressed, the shadow can manifest itself as projections onto others or lead to self-sabotaging patterns. Furthermore, the clash between the conscious ego and the repressed shadow elements often precipitates inner turmoil and dissonance. Understanding the role of the shadow in inner conflicts involves acknowledging its potential to disrupt harmony within the psyche and hinder personal development.

It is essential to integrate the shadow into conscious awareness through a process of introspection, reflection, and self-acceptance. Embracing the shadow entails confronting and assimilating its contents into the wholeness of the psyche, thus promoting inner harmony. Integration of the shadow facilitates the reconciliation of conflicting internal forces, contributing to a more balanced and authentic sense of self. This integration can be a transformative journey marked by increased self-awareness, emotional resilience, and personal growth.

In psychotherapeutic settings, exploring the shadow involves creating a safe and nurturing environment for individuals to confront their hidden aspects openly and without judgment. By engaging in a dialogue with the shadow, individuals can unveil unconscious patterns, unresolved conflicts, and suppressed emotions, fostering a deeper understanding of their inner world. As individuals come to terms with their shadow, they can progress towards a more congruent and empowered state of being, alleviating the inner tensions that arise from the dichotomy between the ego and the shadow.

5. The Integration of Ego and Self:

The journey towards wholeness involves a profound understanding of the interplay between conscious and unconscious aspects of the psyche. As individuals embark on this transformative path, they encounter the inherent conflicts and paradoxes that arise from the coexistence of the ego and self. In essence, holistic development culminates in the harmonious integration of these two fundamental elements, fostering a state of inner equilibrium and self-realization.

Central to the integration of ego and self is the recognition of the shadow, an aspect of the unconscious that embodies repressed or disowned traits and emotions. Embracing the shadow involves confronting and assimilating these suppressed facets, thereby reconciling conflicting elements within the psyche. Through this process, individuals attain a more comprehensive awareness of their psychological landscape, paving the way for genuine self-acceptance and authenticity.

Furthermore, holistic development necessitates the exploration of archetypal patterns that manifest within the individual psyche. These universal symbols hold profound significance in shaping an individual's experiences, behaviors, and perceptions. By engaging with these archetypal forces, individuals gain insights into the profound connection between personal development and collective human experiences, thereby fostering a deeper sense of purpose and meaning.

A crucial aspect of integrating the ego and self revolves around cultivating self-awareness and introspection. Engaging in practices such as meditation, journaling, and reflective contemplation enables individuals to delve into the depths of their psyche, fostering a heightened understanding of the dynamics at play within themselves. This introspective journey serves as a catalyst for embracing and integrating the multifaceted aspects of the ego and self, ultimately leading to a more cohesive and integrated sense of identity.

Inherent in the process of holistic development is the importance of therapeutic interventions that facilitate the reconciliation and unification of the ego and self. Psychotherapeutic approaches, such as Jungian analysis, offer individuals a supportive framework for delving into their inner conflicts and integrating disparate aspects of their psyche. Through the guidance of a skilled therapist, individuals embark on a transformative journey towards achieving inner harmony and self-integration, transcending limitations imposed by unresolved inner conflicts.

6. Therapeutic Approaches for Resolving Inner Conflicts:

Therapeutic approaches for resolving inner conflicts are rooted in the understanding of the complex interplay between the ego and the self within an individual's psyche. The process of integrating the often opposing forces of the ego and the self requires a multidimensional approach that draws upon various psychological theories and practices.

One of the fundamental therapeutic strategies used in resolving inner conflicts is psychoanalysis, which provides a deep exploration of the unconscious mind and its influence on a person's behavior and emotions. By delving into the hidden layers of the psyche, individuals can gain insight into their internal struggles and begin to work towards achieving a harmonious balance between their ego and self.

Additionally, cognitive-behavioral therapy (CBT) offers practical techniques to help individuals identify and challenge maladaptive thought patterns and behaviors associated with inner conflict. Through CBT, individuals can develop coping mechanisms and constructive responses to manage the challenges presented by conflicting aspects of their psyche.

Mindfulness-based approaches, such as mindfulness meditation and acceptance and commitment therapy (ACT), play a significant role in addressing inner conflicts by fostering self-awareness and promoting present-moment experiences. These techniques enable individuals to observe their thoughts and feelings without judgment, leading to greater clarity and acceptance of their inner turmoil.

Another valuable therapeutic modality for resolving inner conflicts is psychodynamic therapy, which focuses on exploring how past experiences and unresolved emotional conflicts impact an individual's present state of being. By unearthing the underlying sources of inner tension, individuals can gain deeper understanding and facilitate the integration of their ego and self.

Humanistic-existential therapies, including person-centered therapy and existential therapy, emphasize the exploration of an individual's authentic self and the pursuit of meaning and purpose. These approaches encourage individuals to delve into their existential dilemmas and confront the core essence of who they are, offering profound insights into resolving inner conflicts.

## Identity in the Context of Jungian Theory

1. Historical Context and Evolution of Identity Concepts:

The concept of identity has been a subject of immense interest throughout human history, with its significance evolving over time. The historical trajectory of identity can be traced back to ancient philosophical and religious traditions, where notions of self-realization, individuation, and the integration of the psyche were explored. These early explorations laid the groundwork for the conceptualization of identity as a complex and multifaceted construct. Furthermore, the emergence of psychological theories in the late 19th and early 20th centuries, particularly the works of pioneers such as Sigmund Freud and Carl Jung, brought forward new dimensions to the understanding of identity. During this period, the focus shifted towards the unconscious and the role of archetypes in shaping individual identity. As psychology continued to advance, the influence of sociocultural factors on identity formation became a prominent area of study. The impact of historical events, societal norms, and cultural narratives on the construction of personal and collective identity added depth to the discourse. Moreover, the postmodern era saw a reevaluation of identity in the wake of globalization, technological advancements, and diverse cultural exchanges. This led to an increased emphasis on the fluidity and multiplicity of identities, challenging traditional views of a unitary and stable self. In contemporary times, the evolution of identity concepts continues to be shaped by ongoing social, political, and technological changes, presenting new complexities and opportunities for exploration.

2. Identity Through the Jungian Lens:

From a Jungian perspective, the notion of identity is not merely confined to individual traits or external roles, but rather extends into the web of the collective unconscious and archetypal patterns that shape one's sense of self. According to Jung, an individual's identity is shaped by a complex interplay of conscious experiences, unresolved conflicts, and the manifestations of the unconscious, all of which work in tandem to influence an individual's perceptions, behaviors, and relationships. Central to Jung's approach is the acknowledgment of the multifaceted nature of identity, which surpasses the confines of rationality and embraces the enigmatic aspects of human existence. This holistic perspective posits that genuine self-discovery and understanding necessitate delving into the depths of the unconscious, where repressed emotions, unacknowledged desires, and forgotten memories reside. Furthermore, Jung emphasizes the dynamic, evolving nature of identity, asserting that it is shaped not only by an individual's personal history but also by the collective narratives, symbols, and myths that permeate the cultural and societal fabric. Unraveling the layers of identity in the Jungian paradigm involves exploring the domains of archetypes, symbolic representations, and the perpetual quest for integration and wholeness. Within this context, personal identity becomes linked to the universal themes and patterns that have resonated throughout human history, transcending temporal and spatial boundaries. The profound impact of Jung's theories on identity is manifested in their ability to provide a comprehensive framework for understanding the complexities inherent in human nature and the rich tapestry of individual and collective identities. Through the lens of Jungian psychology, the journey towards self-realization and authentic identity entails embracing the paradoxes, contradictions, and latent potentials within one's psyche, leading to a deeper appreciation of the interconnectedness of all dimensions of the self and the broader human experience.

3. Identity Formation and Transformation in Jungian Theory:

According to Jung, identity is not fixed or static but rather a dynamic process that unfolds throughout one's life. Central to Jungian theory is the idea of individuation, which refers to the lifelong journey towards wholeness and self-realization. Individuation encompasses the integration of various aspects of the psyche, including both the personal and collective unconscious, leading to the emergence of a more complete and authentic identity. This process of individuation involves confronting and reconciling the different archetypal forces within the unconscious, thereby fostering psychological growth and transformation. Jung believed that the failure to address these deep-seated psychological conflicts could lead to a fragmented identity and psychological distress. Another key aspect of identity formation in Jungian theory is the role of the persona, or the social mask that individuals present to the outside world. The persona serves as a necessary adaptation to societal norms and expectations but can also obscure the true self, making it essential for individuals to differentiate between their social persona and their authentic identity. Further, the exploration of the shadow, representing the hidden and repressed aspects of one's personality, is integral to understanding identity transformation. Embracing and integrating the shadow is fundamental to achieving greater self-awareness and psychological balance. Through the process of engaging with the shadow, individuals can unravel internal conflicts and acknowledge the complexity of their identity, paving the way for personal growth and transformation. Moreover, the dynamic interplay between the anima and animus, representing the feminine and masculine aspects within the psyche, plays a pivotal role in identity development. Understanding and integrating these polarities can lead to a more balanced and harmonious sense of self. Identity transformation in Jungian theory encourages individuals to explore the deeper layers of their psyche, confront internal dichotomies, and seek harmony between conflicting aspects of their identity.

4. Comparison with Freudian Views on Identity:

While both Jung and Freud have significantly influenced the understanding of human identity, their perspectives diverge on various crucial aspects. Freud's conceptualization of the psyche revolves around the id, ego, and superego, wherein he emphasizes the role of the unconscious mind in shaping personality. In contrast, Jung's focus on the collective unconscious, archetypes, and individuation presents a different paradigm for comprehending identity.

One of the fundamental disparities between the two theorists lies in their interpretation of the unconscious. Freud posited that the unconscious is primarily the repository of repressed desires and traumatic experiences, steering individual behavior and mental processes. On the other hand, Jung expanded the notion of the unconscious to encompass not only personal experiences but also inherited symbols and patterns shared by all humanity—the collective unconscious. This broader perspective suggests a more universal understanding of identity formation, one that extends beyond personal conflicts and incorporates archetypal symbols that resonate across cultures and epochs.

Freud's emphasis on the Oedipus complex as a critical determinant of identity development differs from Jung's concept of individuation. While Freud emphasizes the resolution of internal conflicts rooted in childhood experiences, Jung proposes a process of self-realization through the integration of the conscious and unconscious aspects of the psyche. This differentiation elucidates contrasting pathways in addressing identity struggles: Freudian psychoanalysis centers on resolving past traumas, while Jungian therapy focuses on embracing and integrating the unconscious elements to achieve wholeness.

Another crucial aspect of differentiation is found in the interpretations of dreams and symbols. Freud viewed dreams as wish-fulfillment manifestations rooted in unconscious desires, often with sexual undertones. In contrast, Jung regarded dreams and symbols as gateways to the collective unconscious, populated by archetypal figures and motifs that provide profound insights into the individual's journey towards self-discovery and identity realization.

5. The Role of Symbols and Myths in Understanding Identity:

Symbols and myths play a profound role in shaping our understanding of personal and collective identity. In the sphere of Jungian psychology, symbols are regarded as potent carriers of meaning that transcend conscious thought and connect individuals to universal archetypes. These archetypal symbols emerge from the collective unconscious and provide a framework for understanding the deep layers of human identity.

Mythology, as a repository of ancient narratives and symbols, offers invaluable insights into the human psyche and its complex relationship with identity. Myths serve as cultural manifestations of archetypal themes, reflecting universal patterns of human experience and development. Through the study of myths, individuals can gain a deeper understanding of the symbolic language that underpins their personal identity constructs.

Jung emphasized the significance of symbols and myths in unraveling the intricacies of the human psyche and its quest for individuation. By analyzing recurring symbols and mythological motifs, individuals can embark on an introspective journey to unearth the profound layers of their own identity. Moreover, the exploration of symbols and myths serves as a bridge between the conscious and unconscious aspects of identity, fostering greater self-awareness and integration.

The interpretation of symbols and myths is not confined to individual introspection; they also hold relevance in the broader context of societal identity and cultural evolution. As societies evolve, the reinterpretation and re-emergence of ancient symbols and myths reflect the collective endeavor to make sense of the changing world and the underlying human experience. Symbolic representations embedded in art, literature, and rituals offer a rich tapestry through which identities are expressed, reaffirmed, and transformed.

In contemporary society, the revival and reinterpretation of ancient symbols and myths continue to shape identity narratives and foster a sense of belonging and connection across diverse cultural landscapes. The integration of these symbolic elements into therapeutic practices and creative expressions provides avenues for individuals to engage with their identity construction in meaningful ways.

6. Identity Crisis and Psychological Integration

The concept of identity crisis has been a focal point in psychological discourse, especially within the framework of Jungian theory. Identity crisis refers to a period of intense internal conflict and confusion regarding one's self-concept, values, and role in the world. In the context of Jungian psychology, identity crisis often arises when an individual encounters discrepancies between their conscious ego identity and the unconscious aspects of the self, including repressed or unrecognized emotions, desires, and archetypal influences.

Psychological integration, according to Jungian theory, is the process of reconciling these conflicting elements within the psyche to achieve a cohesive and authentic sense of self. This integration involves exploring the shadow aspects of the personality, confronting unresolved traumas, and acknowledging the presence of archetypal forces in shaping one's identity. By addressing these facets, individuals can embark on a transformative journey towards wholeness and psychological well-being.

The manifestation of identity crisis can vary widely, encompassing feelings of alienation, existential angst, or a pervasive sense of inner emptiness. Such experiences often prompt individuals to seek psychological support or therapeutic intervention to explore the layers of their psyche. Jungian-oriented therapy provides a conducive environment for individuals to engage with their unconscious material, explore the symbolic imagery present in their dreams, and examine the archetypal patterns that influence their identity formation.

Crucial to the process of psychological integration is the establishment of a harmonious relationship between the conscious ego and the broader aspects of the self. This involves recognizing and integrating the shadow - the repository of repressed impulses, fears, and unrealized potentials. Through this exploration, individuals can embrace and transcend the conflicts arising from the tension between opposites, leading to a more balanced and resilient sense of identity.

Furthermore, the journey towards integration may involve engaging with creative expressions, such as art, music, or literature, as a means of symbolic representation and catharsis. These modalities provide avenues for accessing the unconscious and expressing its contents in a tangible form, aiding in the process of psychological transformation and identity consolidation.

7. Practical Implications of Jung's Theories on Modern Identity Issues:

Jung's emphasis on the individual's quest for self-discovery and integration provides a framework for managing the complexity of contemporary identity challenges. One practical implication of Jungian theory lies in its application to understanding and addressing cultural and societal influences on identity formation. By recognizing the impact of social norms, media, and technology on the psyche, individuals can gain insight into the shaping of their identities and adopt a more conscious approach to self-realization. Moreover, Jungian concepts such as archetypes and the collective unconscious offer a valuable perspective on the universality of human experiences, transcending cultural boundaries and fostering empathy and understanding in diverse societies. Additionally, Jung's emphasis on the shadow and the integration of repressed aspects of the self has profound implications for addressing issues of identity fragmentation and inner conflict in the modern world. Through therapeutic practices informed by Jungian principles, individuals are empowered to confront and reconcile with their shadow selves, leading to a more holistic and authentic sense of identity. Furthermore, the concept of individuation, central to Jung's theory, provides a roadmap for personal growth and fulfillment in an age marked by rapid societal change and existential uncertainty. By embracing the journey towards self-realization and actualization, individuals can manage identity crises and find meaning in an ever-changing world. From a clinical perspective, Jungian psychology offers practical tools for mental health professionals to engage with and support individuals grappling with identity-related challenges. Therapeutic modalities rooted in Jungian principles facilitate a deeper exploration of the psyche, enabling individuals to uncover and integrate fragmented aspects of their selves. By incorporating techniques such as dream analysis, active imagination, and symbol work, therapists can guide clients towards a more profound understanding of their identities and assist in the process of transformation and healing. In conclusion, the practical implications of Jung's theories on modern identity issues are far-reaching, offering invaluable insights and interventions for individuals, communities, and mental health practitioners. By embracing the richness and depth of Jungian psychology, society is better equipped to manage the complexities of contemporary identity formation and foster a culture of introspection, authenticity, and psychological well-being.

## The Dynamics of Transformation

1. The Role of Dreams in Psychological Transformation:

Dreams have long been regarded as windows into the unconscious mind. From a psychoanalytical perspective, dreams play a crucial role in the process of psychological transformation. Sigmund Freud famously referred to dreams as the 'royal road to the unconscious,' emphasizing their significance in unraveling repressed desires, fears, and unresolved conflicts. In the context of Jungian psychology, dreams are seen as symbolic expressions of archetypal imagery and collective unconscious influences, providing valuable clues for self-discovery and personal growth. Furthermore, contemporary research in neuroscience and cognitive psychology has shed light on the physiological and cognitive mechanisms underlying dream formation and its potential impact on emotional processing and memory consolidation. Therefore, understanding the role of dreams in psychological transformation necessitates a holistic exploration encompassing psychoanalytic, Jungian, and neuroscientific perspectives. When exploring the role of dreams in psychological transformation, it is essential to consider the symbolic nature of dream content. Symbolic interpretation is fundamental to unlocking the underlying meanings and messages embedded within dreams. Through a psychoanalytical lens, dreams are viewed as manifestations of unconscious conflicts, desires, and unresolved issues. By delving into the symbolism present in dreams, individuals can gain insight into their psychodynamic struggles and explore pathways to inner change. Moreover, Jungian psychology emphasizes the collective nature of certain dream symbols, highlighting their relevance to universal human experiences and the archetypal patterns found within the collective unconscious. The fluid and often elusive nature of dream imagery challenges individuals to engage in introspective reflection and undergo a transformative journey of self-discovery. Importantly, the significance of dreams extends beyond mere symbolism. Neuroscientific research has revealed the role of dreams in emotional processing, memory consolidation, and creative problem-solving. During the rapid eye movement (REM) stage of sleep, when dreams predominantly occur, neural networks associated with emotional regulation and memory retrieval are activated, facilitating the integration of emotional experiences and the consolidation of newly acquired knowledge. This neurological foundation underscores the potential of dreams to catalyze psychological transformation by facilitating adaptive emotional processing and promoting cognitive restructuring. Furthermore, studies have demonstrated that dream analysis within therapeutic settings can contribute to enhanced self-awareness, insight, and emotional resolution, thereby fostering psychological well-being and transformative growth. As such, the role of dreams in psychological transformation transcends the scope of symbol and imagination, encompassing a multidimensional interplay of unconscious processes, emotional regulation, and cognitive integration.

2. Symbolic Interpretation - Pathways to Inner Change:

The interpretation of symbols offers a profound pathway to inner transformation within the psychoanalytical framework. Symbolic interpretation delves into the subconscious, bringing to light the hidden meanings and desires that shape an individual's psyche. In this process, symbols are seen as manifestations of unconscious content, and their analysis becomes a powerful tool for understanding and facilitating change. The symbolic language of dreams, fantasies, and creative expressions provides rich material for uncovering the depths of the human mind. Through careful analysis and exploration, these symbols offer pathways to accessing and integrating aspects of the self that lay beyond conscious awareness.

When engaging in symbolic interpretation, the focus is not merely on the literal meaning of the symbol, but rather on its associative and emotional implications. Each symbol carries personal significance, influenced by the individual's unique experiences, cultural background, and archetypal patterns. By deciphering these symbols, individuals can gain insights into their unresolved conflicts, unmet needs, and dormant potential. This process fosters self-awareness and paves the way for meaningful shifts in thought, behavior, and emotional responses.

Symbolic interpretation serves as a bridge between the conscious and unconscious spheres, allowing individuals to explore their inner landscapes with depth and nuance. Symbols often serve as messengers from the unconscious, conveying messages that call for attention and integration. By embracing these symbols with curiosity and openness, individuals embark on a transformative journey, unraveling layers of meaning and fostering psychological growth. This deep introspective work enables individuals to confront and resolve inner conflicts, ultimately leading to a greater sense of wholeness and authenticity.

The therapeutic application of symbolic interpretation holds immense value in the context of psychoanalysis. By engaging in dialogue with trained analysts, individuals can explore the multifaceted dimensions of their symbolic content, gaining new perspectives and reframing their lived experiences. Together, the analyst and the individual collaboratively unpack the symbolic language, uncovering the intricacies of the unconscious to facilitate healing and evolution. This collaborative exploration cultivates trust, empathy, and insight, creating a supportive environment for individuals to embark on transformative journeys.

3. Mechanisms Underlying Psychodynamic Shifts:

Psychodynamic shifts refer to the complex processes that occur within an individual's psyche, leading to significant changes in thought patterns, emotions, behaviors, and overall psychological well-being. These shifts are rooted in the deep layers of the unconscious mind and are influenced by a multitude of factors, including past experiences, internal conflicts, and innate drives. Understanding the mechanisms underlying these transformative processes is crucial for psychoanalysts and individuals seeking personal growth and self-awareness.

At the core of psychodynamic shifts lies the concept of repressed memories and desires. Sigmund Freud's theory of the unconscious mind postulates that traumatic experiences and unresolved conflicts are pushed into the unconscious, where they continue to influence an individual's thoughts and behaviors. Through skilled therapeutic intervention, these repressed elements can be brought into conscious awareness, initiating a fundamental shift in perception and understanding. This process, known as catharsis, allows individuals to release pent-up emotions and gain insight into their inner workings, ultimately paving the way for psychological healing and transformation.

Another essential mechanism is the role of defense mechanisms in shaping psychodynamic shifts. When faced with threatening or distressing thoughts and emotions, individuals often employ various defense mechanisms to protect themselves from psychological harm. These defenses, such as repression, denial, and projection, serve as shields against anxiety-provoking stimuli but can also impede personal growth and hinder authentic self-expression. Recognizing and dismantling these defense mechanisms through therapy can lead to profound shifts in perception and behavior, fostering emotional maturity and enhanced resilience.

The emergence of transference and countertransference dynamics within the therapeutic relationship plays a pivotal role in catalyzing psychodynamic shifts. Transference occurs when patients unconsciously project feelings and attitudes onto their therapists based on past experiences, while countertransference pertains to the therapist's emotional response to the patient. By exploring and managing these complex relational dynamics, individuals can gain deeper insights into their interpersonal patterns and unresolved conflicts, thus propelling transformative change.

In addition, the integration of new insights and perspectives through dream analysis and active imagination serves as potent catalysts for psychodynamic shifts. The symbolic language expressed in dreams and fantasies contains valuable information about an individual's unconscious processes. Engaging with and interpreting these symbols can unravel deeply rooted psychological barriers and open avenues for profound personal growth and transformation.

4. Ego vs. Self - Influences on Personal Growth:

The interplay between the ego and the self holds a pivotal role in the process of personal growth and psychological transformation. The ego, as proposed by Freudian psychoanalysis, represents the conscious aspect of one's identity that interacts with the external world. It is responsible for mediating between inner desires, societal norms, and reality. In contrast, the self, a central concept in Jungian psychology, encompasses the totality of the psyche, including both conscious and unconscious elements. Understanding the dynamic relationship between these two constructs offers profound insights into the mechanisms driving personal development and individuation. The ego, driven by the pursuit of individual desires and the need for social validation, often encounters conflicts with the self, which strives for wholeness and integration of the unconscious aspects. This conflict presents a critical juncture for personal growth, as individuals manage the tension between pursuing their ego-driven aspirations and striving for alignment with their deeper, authentic self. Furthermore, the ego-Self axis influences an individual's capacity for self-reflection, resilience in the face of adversity, and openness to transformative experiences. A harmonious balance between these forces fosters psychological well-being and promotes the emergence of a more integrated and authentic self. Throughout history, literature, mythology, and religious scriptures have depicted narratives that symbolize the eternal struggle between the egoic desires and the transcendence of the self. By exploring these archetypal themes, individuals can gain profound insights into their own inner conflicts and the transformative potential inherent in such struggles. Moreover, psychotherapeutic approaches often focus on integrating the ego and the self, aiming to facilitate an individual's journey towards wholeness and authenticity. Techniques such as dream analysis, active imagination, and the exploration of archetypal motifs serve to bridge the gap between the ego's conscious demands and the self's unconscious wisdom.

5. Jungian Frameworks and Transformative Processes:

In Jungian frameworks, transformative processes are symbolized and facilitated through the exploration of archetypes. Archetypes, being universal patterns or motifs residing in the collective unconscious, provide a framework for understanding the dynamics of personal growth and transformation. These archetypal images manifest in dreams, fantasies, and myths, serving as guides for individuals on their transformative journeys.

The process of transformation within the Jungian framework emphasizes the transcendent function, where the conscious mind engages in an active dialogue with the unconscious. Through this dialogue, conflicts and contradictions are brought to light, leading to the potential for psychological growth and transformation. This transformative process often involves confronting and integrating aspects of the self, including the shadow, anima/animus, and other archetypal manifestations.

The concept of the 'self' as the center of the psyche is integral to Jungian transformative processes. The self represents the archetype of wholeness and integration, and the journey toward wholeness lies at the core of the transformative process. Engaging with the self involves finding harmony and balance amidst the various conflicting elements within the psyche, ultimately leading to a state of psychological equilibrium and individual completeness.

Jungian transformative processes encompass the idea of active imagination, a method through which individuals actively engage with their inner symbolic world. By engaging in active imagination, individuals can access the transformative power of the unconscious and initiate an ongoing dialogue between the conscious ego and the unconscious psyche, thus facilitating the integration of various psychic contents.

6. Stages of Transformation:

Transformation is a complex process that unfolds in distinct stages, marked by significant psychological shifts and internal reorganizations. These stages provide a roadmap for individuals charting their paths toward achieving personal growth and self-realization.

The first stage is often characterized by a profound sense of dissonance and disillusionment with one's current state of being. This disquietude serves as a catalyst for embarking on the journey of transformation. Individuals may grapple with feelings of unrest, dissatisfaction, or yearning for deeper meaning, prompting them to explore the underlying causes and triggers driving this internal turmoil.

As the process advances, the second stage unfolds, marked by introspection and self-exploration. Here, individuals engage in a deep excavation of their psyche, confronting unresolved wounds, shadow aspects, and buried emotions. This arduous yet essential step involves peeling back layers of conditioning and societal impositions to reveal the authentic core of one's being, fostering a heightened self-awareness.

The third stage entails a pivotal moment of revelation and illumination, wherein individuals gain profound insights into their unconscious dynamics and begin to identify archetypal patterns at play within their psyche. This phase of awakening often coincides with epiphanies, symbolic dreams, and synchronicities that offer glimpses of the interconnectedness between the personal and collective unconscious dimensions.

Following this phase, the fourth stage encapsulates the integration and reconciliation of polarities within the individual. Embracing the myriad facets of the self, including the shadow aspects, empowers individuals to transcend inner conflicts and forge a cohesive sense of identity. This crucial reconciliation fosters a harmonious coalescence of divergent elements, laying the groundwork for inner peace and wholeness.

Finally, the fifth stage heralds the culmination of transformation, characterized by the emergence of an individuated, self-realized individual. Emboldened by newfound integrative insights, individuals embody a balanced synthesis of the ego and self, transcending the confines of conventional personas and embracing a more expansive and authentic way of being. This holistic transformation engenders a profound sense of purpose, creative actualization, and spiritual connectedness, marking the fruition of the transformative journey.

7. Therapeutic Techniques Enhancing Transformation:

Therapeutic techniques play a pivotal role in facilitating and enhancing the process of psychological transformation within the context of psychoanalysis. On the other hand, no single technique fits all, and therapists often tailor their methodologies based on individual needs and clinical assessments.

One of the fundamental therapeutic techniques that contribute to transformation is the utilization of active imagination. As conceptualized by Carl Jung, active imagination involves engaging in a dialogue with unconscious elements through creative expression, such as drawing, painting, or guided visualization. By actively interacting with the contents of the psyche, individuals can access deeper layers of the unconscious, thereby fostering transformative insights and self-discovery.

Additionally, dream analysis stands as another potent tool for promoting psychological transformation. Therapists guide individuals in exploring the symbolic language of their dreams, unveiling subconscious patterns and unresolved conflicts. Integrating dream work into therapy offers a unique avenue for individuals to tap into their inner worlds, unraveling hidden meanings and promoting profound shifts in consciousness.

Another influential technique is the practice of mindfulness and meditation. By cultivating present-moment awareness and non-judgmental acceptance, individuals can develop a deeper understanding of their thoughts and emotions. Through mindfulness practices, individuals gain the capacity to observe their internal experiences without attachment, paving the way for transformative changes in perception and behavior.

The use of psychodrama, a therapeutic approach that incorporates role-playing and dramatic enactment, has been instrumental in fostering transformation. By externalizing internal conflicts and interpersonal dynamics, individuals can engage in cathartic experiences, gaining heightened awareness of their inherent patterns and eliciting emotional release. Psychodramatic interventions provide a space for individuals to reframe their narratives and explore alternative perspectives, ultimately contributing to transformative growth.

Cognitive-behavioral techniques are frequently employed to facilitate transformation by targeting maladaptive thought patterns and behaviors. Cognitive restructuring, behavioral activation, and exposure therapies are applied to challenge and modify entrenched beliefs, alleviate emotional distress, and encourage adaptive coping strategies. These evidence-based interventions empower individuals to disentangle themselves from ingrained patterns and embrace new ways of thinking and acting.

8. Challenges and Opportunities in Pursuing Change:

With change comes the inherent risk of uncertainty, resistance, and fear. Often, individuals encounter internal and external obstacles that impede their progress toward inner growth. It becomes imperative to address these challenges and recognize the potential opportunities that lie within. One of the primary challenges is facing the resistance from within one's own psyche. The deeply ingrained patterns and defense mechanisms tend to obstruct the path towards change. Additionally, external factors such as societal norms, familial expectations, and cultural influences can pose significant barriers to embracing transformation. Disentangling oneself from these complex entanglements requires a thorough understanding of the self and a commitment to the process of individuation. Moreover, the fear of the unknown and the loss of familiar structures can be daunting, leading to reluctance in pursuing change. On the other hand, within these challenges, lie abundant opportunities for personal development and growth. When confronting and working through the challenges, individuals have the chance to cultivate resilience, strength, and adaptability. The process of transformation provides an opportunity for individuals to gain deeper insights into their internal dynamics and unearth untapped potential. Furthermore, it offers the prospect of renegotiating one's relationship with oneself and others, fostering new perspectives, and enhancing emotional intelligence. By embracing the discomfort and uncertainties, individuals can open themselves up to profound personal discovery and self-empowerment. In summary, although the pursuit of change is accompanied by formidable challenges, it also presents numerous opportunities for individuals to expand their self-awareness and evolve toward a more integrated and authentic existence.

## Integration – The Harmonization of the Psyche

1. Introduction to Jungian Integration:

Our consciousness represents merely the tip of the iceberg, with the bulk of mental activity occurring in the hidden depths of the unconscious. This includes repressed emotions, forgotten memories, and latent potential waiting to be unearthed and integrated into conscious awareness. The significance of delving into the unconscious lies in its ability to reveal the underlying dynamics that influence our thoughts, feelings, and behaviors. By gaining insight into these hidden aspects, individuals can embark on a transformative journey towards wholeness and self-realization. Such an endeavor often leads to enhanced authenticity, resilience, and a deeper connection to one's inner truth. Jungian psychologist Carl Jung believed that uncovering and integrating unconscious material is crucial for personal growth and psychological well-being. It offers a pathway for individuals to reconcile their fragmented selves and delve into the reservoir of creativity and wisdom within. The integration of the unconscious is thus instrumental in fostering a more profound sense of purpose, meaning, and fulfillment in life. This process transcends mere symptom reduction or problem-solving, extending into a profound reorientation of the individual's relationship with themselves, others, and the world at large. As such, the notion of Jungian integration encapsulates not only psychotherapeutic applications but also broader implications for individual development and societal evolution.

2. The Mechanisms of Integration:

Integration, as understood through the lens of Jungian psychology, involves the process of harmonizing and synthesizing the various elements of the psyche. At its core, integration seeks to bridge the conscious and unconscious aspects of an individual's mind, fostering a cohesive sense of self and reducing inner conflict. This multifaceted process operates on several key mechanisms that are essential to comprehend in order to embark on the journey of psychological wholeness.

One fundamental mechanism of integration is the acknowledgment and exploration of the 'shadow,' a concept introduced by Carl Jung to describe the repressed or denied aspects of one's personality. By willingly confronting and integrating the shadow aspects, individuals can gain a deeper understanding of themselves, leading to personal growth and self-realization.

The process of integration often involves engaging with archetypes, which are universally present symbols and patterns residing in the collective unconscious. Through recognizing and integrating these archetypal energies, individuals can access profound insights and tap into reservoirs of creativity and wisdom.

An essential aspect of integration lies in the interpretation of dreams as rich sources of symbolism and meaning. Dream analysis serves as a pathway to the unconscious, offering glimpses into unresolved emotional conflicts, unexplored desires, and unacknowledged aspects of the self. By delving into dream symbolism, individuals can discern underlying patterns and uncover latent potentials for self-integration.

Additionally, integrating the unconscious necessitates a thoughtful examination of one's defenses and coping mechanisms. By identifying and dismantling maladaptive defense mechanisms, individuals create space for a more authentic and integrated experience of their emotions and experiences. Opening up to vulnerability and embracing authenticity becomes a pivotal aspect of the integration process.

The therapeutic relationship plays a crucial role in the mechanisms of integration. A skilled therapist provides a nurturing and supportive environment for individuals to explore their unconscious depths, examine internal conflicts, and work towards reconciliation and integration. The therapeutic alliance becomes a catalyst for transforming fragmented aspects of the self into a comprehensive and unified whole.

3. Symbolism in Dreams:

In the field of Jungian psychology, dreams are viewed as potent gateways to the unconscious, offering profound insights into the innermost workings of the psyche. Within the tapestry of our dreams lie symbolic representations that serve as conduits for understanding and integrating the unconscious. Jung emphasized that symbols in dreams are not mere random images but meaningful manifestations of underlying emotions, experiences, and archetypal patterns.

The interpretation of dream symbolism requires a nuanced understanding of the personal and collective unconscious, where archetypes reside and influence our perceptions and behaviors. These symbols possess a universal quality, transcending individual experiences and connecting with humanity's shared reservoir of primordial imagery. By unveiling the symbolisms embedded within dreams, individuals gain access to the rich tapestry of their own subconscious, shedding light on repressed thoughts, unresolved conflicts, and unacknowledged desires.

Dreams often present allegorical narratives that reflect an individual's ongoing psychological journey, providing valuable insights into their personal growth and individuation process. Engaging with the symbolism in dreams allows individuals to explore the depths of their unconscious, fostering self-awareness and facilitating integration of previously overlooked elements of the psyche. It is through deciphering these symbols that one can discern the interconnected threads weaving through the conscious and unconscious dimensions, illuminating the dynamics at play within the human mind.

Recognizing the symbolism in dreams empowers individuals to confront their shadow aspects and embrace the totality of their being. By delving into the symbolic motifs that emerge during sleep, individuals can confront suppressed emotions and unexplored facets of the self, catalyzing transformative inner work. This process of engaging with dream symbolism aligns with the broader aim of Jungian integration, wherein the conscious and unconscious become harmoniously unified, fostering wholeness and individuation.

4. Techniques for Facilitating Integration:

Integrating the unconscious is a delicate and complex process that requires a multifaceted approach. Various techniques can be employed to facilitate this integration, each tailored to the individual's unique psyche. One effective technique is active imagination, a method in which individuals engage in a form of conscious fantasy or inner dialogue with the contents of their unconscious. Through active imagination, individuals can bring unconscious material into consciousness, fostering a deeper understanding and integration of their inner world. Another powerful technique is dream analysis, where the symbolism and narratives within dreams are decoded to reveal unconscious dynamics and patterns. By exploring the rich imagery of dreams, individuals gain insight into their unconscious conflicts and desires, paving the way for integration. Additionally, journaling and self-reflection serve as valuable tools for integrating the unconscious.

Through introspective writing and contemplation, individuals can explore their inner thoughts, emotions, and experiences, leading to increased awareness and harmonization of their conscious and unconscious aspects. Furthermore, somatic experiencing and body-centered practices can aid in integrating unconscious material stored in the body. Techniques such as mindfulness, yoga, and breathwork provide avenues for individuals to connect with and release unconscious tensions and traumas held within the body, promoting holistic integration. Moreover, creative expression, such as art therapy, music therapy, and movement-based activities, offers an outlet for the unconscious to manifest symbolically and be integrated through non-verbal means, allowing for a deeper exploration of the inner self. Lastly, psychotherapy and counseling play a pivotal role in facilitating integration. The therapeutic relationship provides a supportive and safe environment for individuals to explore their unconscious material, gain insights, and work through emotional challenges, ultimately contributing to the integration of the unconscious into conscious awareness.

5. The Therapeutic Relationship:

The therapeutic relationship forms the foundation for an individual's journey towards wholeness and self-realization. Within the Jungian framework, the therapist-client relationship is regarded as a crucial vessel through which unconscious material can be explored, understood, and ultimately integrated. Central to this concept is the establishment of trust and rapport, as the client must feel safe and secure in order to explore and confront the depths of their psyche. Through empathetic understanding and active listening, the therapist creates a supportive environment that encourages the expression of unconscious content, facilitating the process of integration.

In addition to providing a safe space, the therapist serves as a knowledgeable guide on the terrain of the unconscious. Drawing from the vast wealth of Jungian theory and practice, the therapist offers valuable insights into archetypal patterns, dream symbolism, and the individuation process, empowering the client to manage the complexities of their inner world with guidance and wisdom. Through this process, the therapeutic relationship becomes a dynamic exchange where the client gains self-awareness and the tools necessary for integration, while the therapist witnesses the unfolding of the client's unique journey towards wholeness.

The therapeutic relationship functions as a mirror, reflecting and elucidating aspects of the client's psyche that may be obscured or overlooked. By providing feedback and interpretations, the therapist helps the client gain clarity and insight into their unconscious material, illuminating shadow elements and fostering a deeper understanding of the self. This reflective aspect of the therapeutic relationship encourages the client to confront internal conflict, embrace disowned aspects of the self, and work towards unification and harmony within the psyche.

The therapeutic relationship is characterized by a profound sense of mutuality and collaboration. Rather than a one-sided interaction, the therapeutic alliance involves a joint exploration of the client's inner landscape, where both therapist and client contribute to the process of integration. The client brings forth their lived experiences, dreams, and fantasies, while the therapist provides a framework for interpretation and analysis. This collaborative engagement fosters a sense of empowerment within the client, enabling them to take an active role in their own psychic transformation.

6. Challenges in the Integration Process:

The journey of integrating the unconscious into conscious awareness is undoubtedly a profound and transformative undertaking, yet it is not without its challenges. One of the primary challenges is the resistance manifested by the ego, which often perceives the integration of unconscious material as a threat to its established identities and defenses. This resistance can manifest as fear, denial, or a strong aversion to exploring unfamiliar aspects of the psyche. Additionally, confronting the shadow – the repository of repressed emotions, desires, and experiences – can evoke intense discomfort and emotional turmoil. The process of acknowledging and embracing these darker aspects of the self requires immense courage and may lead to inner conflict and emotional upheaval. Another significant challenge lies in the deciphering of symbolic representations within dreams and fantasies. Interpreting these manifestations of the unconscious demands a nuanced understanding of archetypal imagery and the ability to discern their personal significance. Furthermore, reconciling conflicting archetypal forces within the psyche poses a formidable challenge, as individuals strive to harmonize polarized elements such as the anima and animus. This task necessitates a delicate balance and a willingness to manage the tensions inherent in the human experience. Moreover, the integration process may be impeded by societal and cultural pressures that cast judgment on unconventional or non-conforming aspects of the self. Managing these external influences while striving for authenticity can be an arduous feat. Finally, the lack of adequate support systems and understanding within one's immediate environment can impede the integration process, hindering individuals from fully engaging in this deeply transformative work. These challenges underline the arduous nature of the integration process, emphasizing the need for patience, perseverance, and a supportive environment in managing the complexities of the unconscious. Overcoming these hurdles is pivotal in realizing the profound metamorphosis that comes with the successful integration of unconscious material into conscious awareness.

7. Implications of Integration for Personal Development:

As individuals embark on the journey of self-discovery and incorporate the previously unconscious aspects of their psyche into their conscious awareness, several transformative implications become evident. One of the key implications of integration is the attainment of a more holistic and authentic sense of self. By acknowledging and embracing the shadow aspects of the personality, individuals can achieve a greater sense of wholeness and integrity. This process allows for a more genuine expression of one's true nature, leading to increased self-acceptance and self-compassion.

The integration of unconscious elements often leads to heightened creativity and innovation. By tapping into the depths of the unconscious mind, individuals are able to access a rich source of inspiration and insight that can fuel artistic expression, problem-solving, and innovative thinking. This creative potential, once unleashed through integration, can significantly enrich an individual's life and contribute to personal and professional growth.

In addition, the process of integration fosters emotional resilience and psychological well-being. As individuals confront and integrate repressed emotions and inner conflicts, they develop greater emotional intelligence and resilience. This enhanced emotional stability equips them with the capacity to manage life's challenges with greater ease and grace, fostering a deeper sense of inner peace and contentment.

The integration of the unconscious facilitates the cultivation of empathy and compassion. As individuals come to terms with their own inner struggles and vulnerabilities, they develop a deeper understanding and empathy towards others' experiences. This heightened empathy enables more meaningful and authentic connections in personal relationships, fostering a more compassionate and harmonious social environment.

Additionally, the integrated individual is better equipped to embark on a journey of individuation, transcending the limitations of societal conditioning and cultural norms to discover and embody their unique potential. Through the integration of unconscious elements, individuals gain the courage and clarity required to pursue their authentic path and fulfill their deepest aspirations, contributing to the enrichment of society at large.

## The Shadow – Exploration of the Hidden Self

1. The Roots of Shadow in Jungian Theory:

The development of Jung's theory on the shadow was influenced by various historical, cultural, and philosophical sources. In the late 19th and early 20th centuries, Jung was immersed in the study of mythology, folklore, and religious symbolism, which greatly shaped his understanding of the human psyche.

Jung's explorations into Alchemy, a medieval philosophical and protoscientific tradition, provided valuable insights into the shadow archetype. He recognized alchemical symbolism as a representation of the individuation process, often involving the confrontation with one's own darkness and the integration of opposing elements. Moreover, Jung's fascination with Eastern philosophies and practices, particularly those of Hinduism and Buddhism, further contributed to his formulation of the shadow concept, as these traditions emphasized the importance of embracing the totality of the self, including its darker aspects.

Additionally, the profound impact of Nietzschean philosophy on Jung cannot be overlooked when examining the historical context of the shadow in Jungian theory. Friedrich Nietzsche's exploration of the duality of human nature, the notion of the 'will to power,' and the concept of the 'eternal recurrence' resonated deeply with Jung's understanding of the shadow as a vital component of the psyche that requires acknowledgment and integration.

The sociopolitical backdrop of Jung's time, marked by the upheaval of two world wars and the collective trauma experienced by humanity, played a pivotal role in shaping his theories, including the shadow archetype. Jung's observations of the shadow's manifestation in mass movements, propaganda, and the atrocities of war informed his recognition of the profound impact of repressed and unacknowledged aspects of the human psyche on individual and collective behavior.

2. Definition - More Than Just Darkness:

The concept of the shadow in Jungian psychology delves far deeper than a mere absence of light or positivity. Rather, the shadow represents the unconscious aspect of the personality that contains repressed weaknesses, desires, and resentments, often deemed as negative by societal norms. It is not a simple repository of harmful impulses; it embodies the totality of the individual's unacknowledged, unexplored potential, including positive qualities that have been overlooked or denied. The shadow's influence can manifest in various ways, from self-sabotaging behaviors to recurring interpersonal conflicts. Understanding the intricacies of the shadow requires a nuanced perspective that transcends conventional dichotomies of good and bad. Embracing the shadow involves acknowledging its existence as an essential part of the self, poised to enrich personal growth and achieve greater wholeness. By confronting the shadow, individuals embark on a journey toward self-realization and integration, recognizing that the darkness within holds invaluable insights into their true nature. This process gives rise to profound transformation, leading to the reconciliation of inner conflicts and the alignment of conscious and unconscious aspects. Embracing the shadow necessitates a courageous exploration, inviting individuals to explore the depths of their psyche with openness and compassion. Through this endeavor, individuals can tap into the hidden potential stored within the shadow, harnessing its power to bring about profound healing and personal evolution. It involves a shift from denial and rejection to acceptance and understanding, propelling individuals toward a more authentic and harmonious way of being. As such, defining the shadow entails not only acknowledging its darker facets but also embracing its potential for profound personal growth and self-actualization.

3. Signals and Signs of our Own Shadow:

As we delve into the process of recognizing our own shadow, it becomes essential to discern the signals and signs that indicate its presence. The first step is self-reflection, a practice that demands sincere introspection and a willingness to confront aspects of oneself that may have long been suppressed or overlooked. It involves acknowledging both our conscious behaviors and our subconscious inclinations, which often reveal themselves through dreams, fantasies, and emotional reactions. These subtle cues can act as guideposts, leading us towards a deeper understanding of our shadow. Another crucial aspect of recognizing the shadow is to pay attention to recurring patterns or themes in our relationships and interactions with others. When we find ourselves repeatedly encountering similar challenges or conflicts, it may signify an underlying projection of our own unacknowledged traits onto those around us. This recognition serves as a powerful tool for uncovering the hidden aspects of our psyche that are seeking integration and acceptance. Furthermore, the examination of our triggers and aversions offers valuable insights into the existence of the shadow. The emotions and responses evoked by certain situations can provide valuable clues about the aspects of ourselves that we have disowned or rejected. Additionally, examining cultural and societal taboos can also shed light on elements of the shadow that may reside within us. Exploring topics that provoke discomfort or feelings of shame can reveal hidden facets of our being that yearn for acknowledgement. Engaging in creative practices such as art, writing, or movement can provide an avenue for the expression and exploration of the shadow. These mediums offer a safe space for delving into the depths of our unconscious, allowing repressed emotions and thoughts to surface.

4. The Role of Projection in Shadow Dynamics:

The process of projection occurs when an individual unconsciously ascribes their own unwanted or disowned aspects onto others or external circumstances. In the context of the shadow, projection allows individuals to avoid recognizing and confronting their own darker traits by attributing them to someone else. This can lead to a distorted perception of reality and strained interpersonal relationships. Understanding the role of projection in shadow dynamics enables individuals to embark on a journey of self-discovery and integration. It becomes a crucial step in shining light on the obscured facets of the self. By acknowledging and exploring projected traits, one can begin to unravel the underlying causes and claim ownership of these disavowed aspects. Without confronting projection, individuals may perpetuate internal conflicts and hinder personal growth. In therapeutic settings, addressing projection is fundamental in guiding individuals towards a more authentic understanding of themselves. Therapists help clients recognize their projected elements and encourage them to reclaim these projections as part of their integrated selves. Essentially, recognizing projection prompts individuals to engage in introspective work, fostering a deeper connection with their shadow and promoting psychological wholeness. Moreover, awareness of projection contributes to healthier interrelations, as it diminishes the tendency to blame others for internal struggles.

5. Techniques for Shadow Work:

When it comes to delving into the sphere of shadow work, individuals are often met with a myriad of emotions, fears, and uncertainties. However, in order to truly embark on a journey of self-discovery and integration, one must be equipped with effective techniques, such as:

- Journaling: Journaling serves as an invaluable tool for delving into the depths of our psyche. By consistently recording thoughts, dreams, and emotions, individuals can begin to discern recurring patterns or themes that may point towards unresolved aspects of their shadow. Through introspective writing, one can gradually unravel the layers of the shadow, gaining insight into suppressed emotions and desires.

- Guided Visualization: Utilizing guided visualization techniques can provide a structured approach to confronting the shadow. By creating a safe mental space and visualizing encounters with symbolic representations of the shadow, individuals can begin to confront and engage with the hidden aspects of their psyche.

Through this process, they may gain clarity on repressed issues and identify potential areas for growth and healing.

- Art Therapy: Expressive forms of art, such as painting, drawing, or sculpting, can serve as powerful mediums for exploring the shadow. Art therapy encourages individuals to externalize their inner conflicts and emotions, allowing for a more tangible exploration of the shadow's manifestations. Engaging in artistic expression can unveil unconscious material and foster a deeper connection to the shadow aspects, ultimately leading to greater self-awareness and acceptance.

- Dream Analysis: Dreams often serve as gateways to the unconscious, offering glimpses into the shadow's elusive domain. By keeping a dream journal and reflecting on recurring symbols, characters, or scenarios, individuals can untangle the symbolism embedded within their dreams, shedding light on repressed aspects of their psyche. Through the interpretation of dreams, one can decipher the messages woven within the subconscious, uncovering hidden facets of the shadow.

- Mindfulness and Meditation: Cultivating mindfulness through meditation practices can aid in fostering a non-judgmental awareness of the present moment. By observing thoughts and emotions without attachment, individuals can begin to recognize shadow tendencies and acknowledge their presence without internal conflict. Mindfulness practices enable individuals to develop a compassionate stance towards their shadow, paving the way for eventual integration and transformation.

6. The Therapeutic Encounter:

As practitioners of Jungian psychology, guiding individuals through the complex terrain of their shadow selves is a delicate task. The therapeutic encounter involves exploring the depths of the unconscious, uncovering repressed elements, and aiding in the integration of these aspects into the individual's conscious being. When guiding others through their shadows, it is essential to create a safe and non-judgmental space where clients feel empowered to explore their deepest fears and desires. This process requires a high level of trust and rapport between the therapist and the client, as delving into the shadow can evoke intense emotions and resistance. Therapists must approach this work with humility, empathy, and a deep understanding of the human psyche. It is crucial to hold space for the client's unfolding journey, allowing them to explore their own revelations and insights. Throughout the therapeutic encounter, the therapist acts as a compassionate guide, offering support and insight without imposing interpretations or projections onto the client's experiences. This requires a finely tuned balance of active listening, gentle probing, and empathetic reflection. An integral aspect of guiding others through their shadows is helping the client recognize and take ownership of their projections onto the external world. By illuminating how their unconscious material manifests in their perceptions of others, the therapist supports the client in reclaiming disowned aspects of themselves. Additionally, therapists facilitate the exploration of archetypal motifs and symbolic representations within the client's shadow, providing a framework for understanding and integrating these powerful psychic forces. The therapeutic encounter also involves assisting clients in recognizing the patterns and behaviors that stem from their shadow aspects, ultimately empowering them to make conscious choices in alignment with their true selves. Throughout this process, the therapist holds a space for the client's transformative journey, respecting the individual's pace and readiness for self-discovery and integration.

7. Challenges and Resistances in Embracing the Shadow:

Embracing the shadow, while pivotal for individuation and self-discovery, is a daunting endeavor fraught with challenges and resistances. Upon embarking on the journey of confronting the shadow, individuals may encounter various obstacles that impede their path towards integration and wholeness. Understanding and managing these challenges is crucial for achieving meaningful transformation and personal growth. One of the primary challenges in embracing the shadow is the inherent discomfort associated with acknowledging and accepting one's darker aspects. It often involves delving into repressed emotions, traumatic experiences, and unresolved conflicts, which can evoke intense feelings of vulnerability and fear. This emotional resistance acts as a protective mechanism, as individuals instinctively strive to shield themselves from pain and discomfort. Moreover, societal stigmas and taboos surrounding certain aspects of the shadow, such as anger, aggression, or sexuality, further compound the challenge of accepting these facets of the self. Overcoming these cultural biases requires a concerted effort to redefine and reclaim the shadow without succumbing to external judgment. Beyond emotional and societal barriers, cognitive and psychological resistances also manifest during the process of embracing the shadow. The ego, driven by a desire to maintain stability and control, often opposes the dissolution of its established identity constructs. This resistance stems from the ego's reluctance to relinquish ingrained patterns and beliefs, as well as its aversion to the uncertainty and unpredictability inherent in shadow exploration. Individuals may experience inner conflict and cognitive dissonance as they grapple with the contradictions between their idealized self-image and the confronting realities of their shadow. Furthermore, confronting the shadow necessitates a willingness to challenge deeply entrenched defense mechanisms and coping strategies that have enabled individuals to repress and avoid uncomfortable truths about themselves. Overcoming these psychological defenses demands a profound commitment to self-examination and an openness to exploring the depths of one's psyche. Addressing these resistances calls for patience, compassion, and self-compassion, as individuals traverse the terrain of their inner world. Additionally, the therapeutic alliance plays a pivotal role in supporting individuals as they confront and transcend these hurdles. Therapists must provide a safe and nonjudgmental space for clients to explore their shadow, offering guidance and encouragement as they manage the complexities of their internal landscape. By fostering trust and rapport, therapists facilitate the gradual dismantling of resistances, enabling clients to delve deeper into their shadow material.

**The Persona - A Social Façade**

1. Concept and Its Origins:

The concept of the persona holds a significant place within Jungian theory, emerging as a fundamental element in understanding the complex dynamics of the human psyche. In delving into the persona's origins, it is crucial to acknowledge its connection to Jung's influential concepts of the collective unconscious and archetypes. Jung proposed that the persona represents the social mask or facade that individuals present to the external world, serving as a means of adapting to societal expectations and norms. This concept finds its roots in Jung's deep-seated belief in the existence of an inherent human tendency to create and maintain certain images or personas. Additionally, the persona acts as a mediator between the individual and society, reflecting the interplay between personal identity and the demands of the external environment.

2. Formation of the Persona:

For Jung, the persona is not a static aspect of the psyche but instead develops and evolves over time. Its formation is influenced by a multitude of factors, including societal norms, cultural expectations, and individual experiences. From early childhood, individuals begin to internalize societal ideals and norms, which subsequently shape the development of their persona. This process is further influenced by familial dynamics, educational experiences, and the influence of media and popular culture. As individuals mature, the persona continues to be shaped by interactions with peers, authority figures, and broader social contexts. The development of the persona is often marked by a continuous negotiation between external influences and internal desires, leading to the creation of a facade that aligns with societal expectations while also reflecting elements of the authentic self.

Furthermore, the persona can be deeply intertwined with one's professional identity, as individuals adapt their public image in accordance with occupational requirements and societal standards. The evolutionary nature of the persona necessitates an ongoing exploration of its development, as it can shift and transform in response to life experiences and changing social environments.

3. The Role of the Persona in Social Interactions:

The role of the persona in social interactions is a complex and multifaceted aspect of human behavior. This facet of the psyche, as understood through the lens of Jungian psychology, serves as the interface between an individual and the outside world, often embodying the socially acceptable traits and behaviors that enable successful engagement within various contexts. It acts as a mask or facade that individuals present to others, influencing how they are perceived and received in social settings. Additionally, the persona mediates the individual's expression of their inner thoughts and emotions, shaping their outward demeanor to align with societal norms and expectations. In essence, it functions as a bridge between the private sphere of the self and the public sphere, allowing for the navigation of diverse social landscapes. The persona's characteristic adaptability enables individuals to adjust their behavior and presentation according to the demands of different social environments, thereby facilitating smooth and harmonious interactions. Moreover, its influence extends beyond mere superficial interactions, as the persona also plays a pivotal role in the establishment and maintenance of relationships. By deploying specific facets of the persona tailored to different social settings, individuals can effectively manage and thrive within their personal and professional networks. However, the persona's pervasive influence can potentially lead to complexities in interpersonal dynamics. In some instances, individuals may inadvertently become overly identified with their personas, resulting in a stark misalignment between their authentic selves and their outward presentations. Such instances can give rise to inner conflict and psychological distress, emphasizing the importance of maintaining a healthy balance between the persona and the genuine self. Furthermore, the persona's impact on social interactions underscores the need for introspective reflection and self-awareness to ensure authenticity and congruence in interpersonal engagements.

4. Persona vs. Self:

From a Jungian perspective, the persona represents the social mask or facade that individuals present to the external world. In elucidating the understanding of the persona, it is crucial to differentiate it from the core, authentic self, a task that forms the crux of individuation. At its essence, the persona serves as the interface between the inner world and the outer reality, modifying behaviors and expressions to fit societal norms and expectations.

To differentiate between the persona and the self in a Jungian framework, one must delve into the depths of the unconscious and the inherent archetypal patterns that shape human behavior. According to Jung, the self embodies the totality of an individual's psyche, comprising both conscious and unconscious elements. It is the seat of authenticity, representing the unadulterated essence of an individual's being, free from societal conditioning or external influences. Conversely, the persona is the outward projection of the self, influenced by societal norms, cultural mores, and contextual demands.

A key aspect of differentiating between the persona and self lies in recognizing the fluid nature of the persona, which adapts and morphs in response to various environmental stimuli. Whereas the self remains a more stable entity rooted in the depths of the unconscious, the persona is malleable, taking on different guises based on situational demands. This dynamic interplay between the persona and the self often leads to inner conflicts and identity crises, particularly when individuals become overly enmeshed with their personas, losing touch with their authentic selves.

The differentiation between persona and self is instrumental in facilitating the process of individuation, which involves integrating the disparate aspects of the psyche to achieve wholeness and self-realization. Failure to discern between the persona and the self can lead to a state of dissonance, hindering the individual's journey towards individuation and self-actualization. Hence, fostering an awareness of this demarcation is paramount in managing the complexities of the human psyche and fostering psychological well-being.

5. Impact of the Persona on Personal Relationships:

The persona, as a social mask worn in various interpersonal interactions, significantly influences personal relationships. Our choice of persona in different settings affects how we are perceived by others and consequently impacts the dynamics of our relationships. When individuals consistently project a particular persona, it can shape their experiences and connections with others. Moreover, the persona's adaptability plays a pivotal role in adjusting to diverse social scenarios, possibly leading to genuine connections or superficial encounters. The influence of the persona on personal relationships becomes evident in both positive and negative aspects. A well-crafted persona may facilitate favorable initial impressions and smooth social interactions, nurturing harmonious relationships. However, reliance on a facade can hinder authentic connections, hindering the development of genuine intimacy and understanding in relationships. Furthermore, discrepancies between one's true self and the projected persona may lead to misunderstandings, conflict, and emotional distance in relationships. Understanding the impact of the persona on personal relationships is crucial for fostering meaningful and fulfilling connections. Recognizing the balance between authenticity and adaptive social presentation allows individuals to manage relationships with integrity and empathy. By acknowledging the role of the persona in shaping interpersonal dynamics, individuals can strive for sincerity and vulnerability in their interactions, fostering deeper connections. Cultivating self-awareness regarding the personas employed in different contexts empowers individuals to align their outward expressions with inner truth.

6. Adaptive Use of Persona:

Understanding the adaptive use of the persona involves recognizing its capacity for flexibility and change. Individuals often adjust their personas to suit various situations and environments, demonstrating a remarkable ability to adapt to diverse social dynamics. This adaptive quality allows individuals to manage through different roles and expectations, enhancing their social interactions and relationships. The persona serves as a tool for individuals to effectively engage with others while maintaining a sense of authenticity within themselves. However, the adaptive use of the persona requires a delicate balance between adaptation and maintaining genuine expressions of self. When employed skillfully, the persona can facilitate meaningful connections and enrich personal experiences. Moreover, the flexible nature of the persona usage enables individuals to explore new facets of their identities, fostering personal growth and development. In essence, the adaptive use of the persona embraces the fluidity of human interaction and the ever-evolving nature of the self. It empowers individuals to engage authentically with the world while acknowledging the need for adaptation in diverse social settings. This adaptive process encourages individuals to be responsive to change, promoting resilience and agility in managing various social roles and responsibilities. It also underscores the importance of self-awareness and introspection, as individuals continuously evaluate and adjust their personas in alignment with their evolving values and aspirations.

7. Dangers of Over-Identification with the Persona:

Over-identification with the persona, or the external social mask, poses significant risks to an individual's psychological well-being and personal development. When individuals become overly attached to their projected persona, they may experience a disconnection from their true selves, leading to inner conflict and emotional distress. This over-identification can be especially detrimental in interpersonal relationships, as it can hinder genuine connections and create barriers to authentic communication. Moreover, reliance on the persona as a primary mode of interaction can result in a loss of self-awareness and a lack of introspection, perpetuating a cycle of inauthentic behavior and emotional detachment. In addition, over-identification with the persona may lead to an erosion of self-confidence, as individuals become reliant on external validation through the projection of a carefully crafted image. This can ultimately impede personal growth and the pursuit of genuine fulfillment. Furthermore, the prolonged maintenance of a persona that is incongruent with one's inner self can generate feelings of alienation and a sense of inner fragmentation, leading to heightened anxiety, depression, and existential disillusionment. As the individual becomes increasingly disconnected from their authentic identity, they may experience a pervasive sense of emptiness and existential angst. These dangers underscore the importance of recognizing the potential pitfalls of over-identifying with the persona and emphasize the need for fostering congruence between the external presentation and the internal reality. By acknowledging the risks associated with excessive attachment to the persona, individuals can embark on a path of self-discovery and alignment, striving for authenticity and autonomy in their interactions and self-expression. This necessitates a mindful examination of the underlying motivations driving the projection of the persona, as well as a deliberate effort to cultivate self-awareness and acceptance of one's multidimensional nature.

8. A Balance between the Persona and Authenticity:

While the persona serves as a protective mask in social interactions, over-identification with it can lead to a disconnection from one's authentic self. Achieving congruence between the persona and authenticity involves a deep exploration of one's core values, beliefs, and emotions. It requires a willingness to critically examine the roles we play in various social contexts and the genuine motivations behind these roles.

In the pursuit of congruence, individuals must cultivate self-awareness and introspection. This involves embracing vulnerability and acknowledging the existence of conflicting desires and societal pressures. By understanding the origins of the persona and its adaptive function, individuals can consciously align it with their true selves, fostering a sense of harmony and integrity.

Achieving congruence demands courage and resilience. It necessitates a willingness to confront societal expectations and norms, challenging the status quo when it conflicts with personal values. This process often entails stepping beyond comfort zones, daring to express genuine thoughts and emotions, even when they diverge from societal conventions.

An essential aspect of this quest is developing self-compassion and acceptance. Embracing imperfections and contradictions within oneself facilitates an authentic integration of the persona. Striving for congruence does not imply eradicating the persona; rather, it calls for aligning it with one's core identity, transforming it into a genuine reflection of the self.

Case studies reveal the profound impact of achieving congruence between the persona and authenticity. Individuals who successfully harmonize these aspects report heightened self-esteem, improved interpersonal relationships, and a greater sense of purpose and fulfillment. Conversely, those struggling with incongruence often experience internal conflict, emotional distress, and difficulties in establishing meaningful connections.

9. Reflective Practices for Harmonizing Persona and Inner Self:

By introspectively examining the dynamics between the persona and the true self, one can gain a deeper understanding of these elements and work towards achieving greater alignment. Reflective practices serve as a bridge between the conscious and unconscious aspects of the psyche, facilitating a process of self-discovery and integration.

One key reflective practice is journaling, wherein individuals document their thoughts, emotions, and experiences. Through consistent journaling, one can identify recurring patterns in their interactions with others, discerning when the persona may be overly dominant or incongruent with the inner self. This heightened awareness allows individuals to consciously adapt their social behaviors and presentations, fostering a more authentic expression of self.

Meditative practices also play a pivotal role in harmonizing the persona and inner self. By engaging in mindfulness meditation, individuals can observe their thoughts and feelings without judgment, gaining clarity on the motives behind their persona's actions. This heightened self-awareness fosters a sense of internal balance, reducing the need to rely solely on the persona for social interactions.

Seeking feedback from trusted confidants or therapists can provide valuable insights into the congruence between one's persona and authentic self. Constructive feedback enables individuals to recognize blind spots and areas for growth, guiding them towards a more harmonious integration of their external presentation and internal identity.

In addition to individual reflective practices, group dialogue and discussions can be instrumental in managing the complexities of persona-personality integration. Participating in group settings allows individuals to witness diverse perspectives and understand how others perceive their presented personas. This collective awareness promotes empathy and understanding, facilitating the alignment of the persona with the core self.

Ultimately, incorporating these reflective practices into daily life empowers individuals to align their persona with their inner self authentically. By conscientiously exploring and harmonizing the relationship between these components, individuals can cultivate a more cohesive and integrated sense of identity, leading to enriched personal fulfillment and meaningful interactions.

## Anima and Animus - The Gendered Archetypes of Soul

1. Introduction to Animus and Anima Concepts:

The Animus and Anima concepts are fundamental components of Carl Jung's analytical psychology, representing the masculine and feminine archetypes within the human psyche. To comprehend the origins of these concepts, one must delve into the historical context and theoretical foundations of Jungian theory. Carl Gustav Jung, a pioneering figure in the field of psychology, developed these concepts based on his extensive research and clinical observations. Influenced by a myriad of sources, including mythology, religious symbolism, and cross-cultural studies, Jung synthesized these elements to form a cohesive framework for understanding the complexities of human personality. The concept of anima, as the feminine aspect of the male psyche, can be traced back to Jung's early work with dreams and visions, where he identified recurring female figures that seemed to possess intrinsic symbolic significance. Meanwhile, the animus, representing the masculine element within the female psyche, emerged as a parallel construct through Jung's exploration of the unconscious. These seminal ideas were further informed by Jung's interactions with colleagues such as Sigmund Freud and his own introspective experiences. Additionally, Jung drew inspiration from diverse cultural traditions, recognizing universal patterns in the depiction of gender archetypes across different societies and historical periods. This inclusivity and interdisciplinary approach allowed Jung to refine and deepen his understanding of the Animus and Anima, which have since become cornerstones of Jungian psychology. Furthermore, the influence of philosophical and mythological frameworks, particularly from ancient civilizations such as the Greeks and Egyptians, significantly shaped Jung's conceptualization of the Animus and Anima.

2. Historical Context and Theoretical Foundations:

The historical context and theoretical foundations of the Animus and Anima concepts in Jungian psychology are deeply rooted in cultural, mythological, and philosophical traditions. Jung's work was profoundly influenced by his extensive knowledge of mythology, folklore, and religious symbolism from diverse cultures. He drew upon this rich tapestry of human narratives to construct his theory of archetypes, which served as universal prototypes for aspects of human experience. The archetypes of Animus and Anima are deeply intertwined with these cultural narratives and consequently reflect a collective unconscious that transcends individual experiences.

The theoretical foundations of Animus and Anima can be traced back to Jung's broader conceptual framework of the psyche. His emphasis on the existence of both personal and collective unconscious, and the idea of psychic totality, laid the groundwork for understanding the dynamic interplay of masculine and feminine energies within the individual. Moreover, Jung's views on the process of individuation, where the integration of unconscious elements contributes to psychological wholeness, directly inform the understanding of Animus and Anima as pivotal components of this transformative journey. The theoretical lens through which Jung approached these archetypes demonstrates his commitment to synthesizing empirical observations with profound insights from various disciplines, including anthropology, history, and religion.

3. Distinction Between Animus and Anima:

In Jungian psychology, the concepts of animus and anima represent the masculine and feminine aspects within the human psyche, respectively. The animus, as a representative of the masculine principle, embodies traits such as assertiveness, rationality, and logic. It's often portrayed as the inner voice that guides a person towards making decisions rooted in reason and analysis. On the other hand, the anima symbolizes the feminine qualities, encompassing intuition, emotionality, and creativity. It's the source of inspiration and nurturance, guiding individuals to connect with their deeper feelings and express themselves authentically. Distinguishing between animus and anima involves recognizing their distinct characteristics and understanding how they shape the psyche differently. While the animus encourages independence and autonomy, the anima fosters connection and empathy. These archetypes not only exist within each individual but also interact with one another, establishing a complex dynamic that influences one's perceptions and attitudes towards the self and others. As individuals move through life experiences, the interplay between these forces can either create harmony or lead to inner conflicts. Recognizing the manifestations of animus and anima in daily interactions, relationships, and decision-making processes offers invaluable insight into the intricacies of psychological dynamics. Furthermore, differentiating between animus and anima is pivotal in cultivating a balanced and integrated psyche. Embracing both aspects allows individuals to harness the strength of their masculine and feminine energies, leading to a holistic approach to self-discovery and personal growth.

4. Psychological Implications of Animus and Anima:

Jungian theory posits that animus and anima play a pivotal role in shaping an individual's perception of self and others. These archetypes are not mere theoretical constructs but hold significant weight in influencing emotions, behaviors, and relationships. When they remain unconscious or unacknowledged, they can manifest in destructive ways, leading to inner conflicts and relational discord. Understanding the psychological implications of animus and anima is paramount in achieving a balanced and harmonious state of being.

In the context of the anima, it represents the feminine aspect within the male psyche. Its psychological implications can be observed in the way men relate to and perceive women, as well as their attitudes towards sensitivity, emotionality, and nurturing qualities. Unconscious anima projections onto women can lead to idealization or demonization, creating unrealistic expectations and relational challenges. Conversely, the animus, representing the masculine aspect within the female psyche, influences how women relate to masculinity, rationality, assertiveness, and autonomy. Unacknowledged animus projections can lead to power struggles and difficulties in establishing healthy boundaries.

The anima and animus archetypes impact one's capacity for introspection, creativity, and self-expression. The anima's influence often manifests in artistic endeavors, emotional depth, and intuitive insights, while the animus contributes to logical reasoning, problem-solving abilities, and assertive communication. Recognition and integration of these archetypal energies can enrich one's psychological well-being and creative potential.

It's crucial to recognize that the anima and animus exist not only within the individual but also collectively. Societal norms and cultural expectations often influence the manifestation of these archetypes, leading to stereotypical gender roles and biases. By exploring the psychological implications of animus and anima on a collective level, individuals can gain a deeper understanding of how societal constructs impact personal development and interpersonal dynamics.

In therapeutic settings, addressing the psychological implications of animus and anima involves facilitating a process of individuation, where individuals consciously engage with and integrate these archetypal energies. Through dream analysis, active imagination, and other therapeutic techniques, individuals explore the unconscious manifestations of animus and anima, working towards establishing a more balanced and authentic sense of self. Ultimately, embracing the psychological implications of animus and anima leads to greater self-awareness, emotional resilience, and enriched relationships.

5. The Role of Animus in Female Psyche:

Derived from the Latin word for 'soul,' animus embodies aspects of masculinity residing within the female unconscious. These archetypal representations manifest in various forms, often influencing a woman's attitudes, beliefs, and behaviors. At its core, the animus serves as a catalyst for asserting independence, critical thinking, and inner strength within the female psyche. This archetype prompts women to confront societal expectations and emerge as empowered individuals. However, the animus can also evoke challenges if left unexamined, leading to inner turmoil and conflict. The recognition and integration of the animus archetype can result in profound personal development and psychological wholeness. It enables women to embrace both their femininity and the constructive qualities derived from the animus, fostering a harmonious balance within the self. The animus' influence extends beyond individual psychology, permeating interpersonal relationships and societal dynamics. Understanding the animus is instrumental in addressing gender-related issues, facilitating empathy, and promoting gender equality. The animus in the female psyche ultimately represents a source of resilience, wisdom, and empowerment, advocating for the holistic growth and fulfillment of women in diverse contexts.

6. The Influence of Anima in Male Psyche:

Jung postulated that the anima represents the feminine qualities residing within the male unconscious. These qualities encompass a wide spectrum, including nurturing, sensitivity, emotionality, and receptivity. The anima plays a pivotal role in shaping a man's inner world, influencing his relationships, self-perception, and creative expressions. It acts as a bridge between the conscious and unconscious, serving as a guide to the deepest layers of the male psyche.

Jung believed that the anima manifests itself through images and symbols in the male's dreams and fantasies. These manifestations provide valuable insights into the man's emotional and psychological landscape, reflecting the presence and influence of the anima. When a man is disconnected from his anima, he may exhibit behaviors of emotional aloofness, insensitivity, or an exaggerated display of masculinity. Conversely, embracing and integrating the anima can lead to a more balanced and harmonious personality, allowing for greater empathy, creativity, and emotional depth.

It is essential for men to recognize and engage with their anima, as this process enables them to develop a deeper understanding of themselves and their relationships. By acknowledging and integrating the feminine aspects of their psyche, men can experience profound personal growth and transformation. The anima also has implications in romantic relationships, as it influences a man's perceptions and interactions with the opposite sex. Understanding and reconciling with the anima allows men to relate to women with increased empathy, respect, and understanding, contributing to healthier and more fulfilling dynamics.

The anima holds creative potential within the male psyche. By engaging with the anima, men can tap into their intuitive and artistic abilities, fostering innovation and imagination. This process of integration leads to a more holistic expression of masculinity and empowers men to embrace a broader range of emotional experiences and interpersonal connections.

7. The Balancing of Masculine and Feminine Energies Internally:

Traditionally, these two energies have been associated with gender roles, with masculinity linked to assertiveness, rationality, and strength, while femininity is associated with nurturing, empathy, and intuition. However, Jungian theory posits that every individual possesses both masculine and feminine energies regardless of their gender, and an imbalance or repression of either can lead to psychological distress. Achieving internal equilibrium between these energies is crucial for psychological well-being and personal development.

To begin the process of balancing these energies, individuals must first become aware of their own psychological tendencies and biases toward masculine and feminine traits. This self-awareness involves recognizing and acknowledging which aspects are dominant or suppressed within oneself, and understanding how they manifest in different contexts. By exploring the influence of cultural, familial, and societal factors, individuals can gain insight into the origins of their beliefs and attitudes towards gender-specific traits.

Once awareness is established, the next step is to embrace and integrate both masculine and feminine qualities into one's psyche. This integration does not entail erasing or denying one's inherent traits but rather acknowledging and valuing them as essential parts of the self. For instance, an individual may work on nurturing their assertiveness while also cultivating their capacity for empathy and intuition, thereby harmonizing the two energies within themselves.

Achieving balance between masculine and feminine energies encompasses recognizing and reconciling internal conflicts stemming from societal expectations and pressures. Society often imposes rigid standards regarding gender roles, which can exacerbate the dissonance within an individual striving for harmony. By deconstructing societal norms and embracing a more fluid and inclusive view of gender expression, individuals can alleviate the inner conflict caused by external influences.

Ultimately, balancing masculine and feminine energies internally fosters greater psychological resilience, emotional depth, and creative expression. This process enables individuals to tap into a wider array of human experiences and potentials, contributing to a more holistic sense of self and a deeper connection with others. Embracing both masculine and feminine energies not only enhances individual well-being but also enriches interpersonal relationships, fostering mutual understanding and empathy. By attaining internal equilibrium, individuals can authentically express the totality of their being, transcending conventional limitations and embracing a more nuanced and integrated sense of self.

8. Cultural Reflections on Animus and Anima Archetypes:

The anima and animus archetypes have been deeply ingrained in cultural narratives and representations across various civilizations, offering profound insights into the collective expression of masculine and feminine energies. In many ancient mythological traditions, such as Greek, Norse, and Egyptian mythology, we witness personifications of anima and animus through deities, heroes, and heroines. These archetypal manifestations not only reflect the cultural values and norms, but also encapsulate the eternal struggle and interplay between the masculine and feminine aspects of the human psyche. Furthermore, literary and artistic works from different cultures often depict the anima and animus archetypes in symbolic and allegorical forms. For instance, in classic literature, the representation of anima and animus can be observed in characters embodying contrasting gender traits, serving as conduits for exploring human complexities and interpersonal dynamics. Moreover, indigenous traditions and rituals frequently incorporate symbolic practices that honor and integrate the dualistic nature of animus and anima, emphasizing the importance of harmony and balance between these primal forces. By recognizing the pervasive presence of anima and animus in cultural contexts, we acknowledge the enduring significance of these archetypes in shaping human understanding of gender, relationships, and self-realization. The exploration of cultural reflections on animus and anima archetypes not only enriches our comprehension of individual psychological development, but also fosters a broader awareness of the interplay between societal constructs and innate masculine and feminine energies. As such, the integration of cultural perspectives enhances the holistic approach to animus and anima, transcending personal introspection to encompass the broader socio-cultural influences that shape and mold these archetypal forces within the collective human experience.

9. Therapeutic Approaches to Animus and Anima Integration:

Therapeutic approaches to animus and anima integration involves the utilization of psychotherapeutic techniques to aid individuals in harmonizing and integrating their inner masculine and feminine energies, ultimately fostering a sense of wholeness and balance within the psyche. This process is guided by a profound understanding of the archetypal forces at play in shaping an individual's unconscious dynamics. These therapeutic approaches draw from various schools of psychology, including analytical psychology, depth psychology, and psychodynamic therapy, to create a comprehensive framework for addressing anima and animus integration.

The therapist assumes a crucial role in guiding clients through the journey of animus and anima integration. Central to this process is the exploration of the client's unconscious through dream analysis, active imagination, and symbolic interpretation. By unraveling the symbols and manifestations of the anima and animus archetypes within the client's psyche, the therapist assists in illuminating the unconscious content and facilitating conscious awareness. This awareness serves as the cornerstone for initiating the integration process. Additionally, the therapeutic relationship provides a secure container for the client to engage with and understand the masculine and feminine aspects of their being in a non-judgmental and supportive environment.

Therapeutic interventions may encompass the exploration of gender identity and societal influences that shape an individual's relationship with their internal archetypal energies. Techniques such as role-playing, narrative therapy, and exploration of cultural and familial conditioning are employed to unravel the complex interplay between personal experiences and collective influences. By examining societal norms and expectations related to gender roles, clients can gain insight into how these external factors have shaped their anima and animus archetypes, thereby enabling them to manage and integrate these polarities more effectively.

Psychoeducation on anima and animus archetypes forms an integral part of the therapeutic process. Clients are educated about the history and significance of these archetypes, their symbolic representations, and their influence on personal development. Understanding the archetypal nature of anima and animus allows clients to approach the integration process with heightened self-awareness and a deeper comprehension of the transformative potential inherent in embracing their inner dualities.

Ultimately, therapeutic approaches to animus and anima integration bridge the theoretical constructs of Jungian psychology with real-world application in the sphere of healing and personal growth. By providing a structured and supportive environment for clients to explore and integrate their unconscious dynamics, these approaches contribute to the development of a more unified and individuated self.

## STAGES OF INDIVIDUATION

### The Initial Encounter

In the journey of individuation, the initial encounter with the persona represents a critical stage in the process of self-discovery and psychological development. The persona, as defined by Jungian psychology, encompasses the roles we play, the identities we adopt, and the outward characteristics we exhibit to conform to societal expectations and norms. The confrontation with the persona involves a profound exploration of one's genuine self beyond the veneer of social conventions and expectations. This introspective process requires individuals to critically evaluate their beliefs, behaviors, and self-perceptions that have been shaped by external influences. By peeling back the layers of the persona, individuals gain insights into their true nature, aspirations, and intrinsic motivations. This introspective journey often involves moments of dissonance and cognitive dissonance as individuals come face-to-face with the misalignment between their authentic selves and the person they present to others. Additionally, the revelation of the persona's limitations and constraints can induce feelings of vulnerability and uncertainty, compelling individuals to embark on a quest for self-authenticity and self-actualization. As individuals move through this phase, they are challenged to distinguish between socially constructed personas and the essence of their core being. Consequently, this process empowers them to shed societal conditioning and embrace their unique individuality. Furthermore, the confrontation with the persona lays the groundwork for cultivating a deeper understanding of the multifaceted dimensions of the human psyche. By embracing the complexity of the persona and acknowledging its influence, individuals can embark on a transformative odyssey towards personal integration and wholeness. Moreover, this phase exemplifies a pivotal moment for fostering empathy and compassion towards oneself and others, as the nuances of persona dynamics are unveiled through introspection and self-awareness. In conclusion, the initial encounter with the persona marks the commencement of an inward expedition that propels individuals towards profound self-realization, authenticity, and resilience.

**Engagement with the Shadow**

When individuals embark on the journey of individuation, they are confronted with the imperative task of integrating these hidden elements into their conscious awareness. The process of engaging with the shadow is transformative, as it involves acknowledging, accepting, and reconciling with the darker facets of one's personality.

Initially, individuals may resist acknowledging the existence of their shadow, often attributing negative or undesirable traits to external sources. However, through introspection and self-exploration, the shadow gradually unveils itself, demanding recognition and integration. This encounter evokes feelings of discomfort, as it challenges the established self-image and societal expectations. It requires considerable courage and psychological resilience to delve into the depths of the shadow, embracing its complexities without succumbing to denial or evasion.

As individuals commence the process of integrating the shadow, they are compelled to confront unresolved emotions, past traumas, and suppressed desires that have been relegated to the unconscious. Without addressing these repressed elements, individuals remain constrained by their own internal conflicts, inhibiting personal growth and psychological development. Through meticulous introspection and therapeutic interventions, individuals can gradually shed light on the obscured aspects of their shadow, uncovering profound insights into their multifaceted nature.

The integration of the shadow extends beyond personal revelations and encompasses interpersonal dynamics. By acknowledging and assimilating repressed elements, individuals cultivate empathy, compassion, and understanding towards others, recognizing shared vulnerabilities and intrinsic humanity. This transformation transcends the confines of the individual psyche, permeating relationships and fostering profound connections based on authentic acceptance and mutual respect.

In the context of individuation, the engagement with the shadow serves as an essential catalyst for inner transformation, paving the way for greater self-awareness and psychological wholeness. It epitomizes the arduous yet enriching process of synthesizing the fragmented aspects of the self, ultimately contributing to the realization of one's innate potential and authenticity.

### The Balance of Inner Opposites

The encounter with the anima/animus often manifests as projections onto external figures before the internalization and integration process commences. Engaging with the anima/animus entails a deep introspective journey, requiring individuals to confront stereotypical gender norms and predefined societal constructs. It involves recognizing and embracing qualities that are traditionally associated with the opposite gender, thereby fostering an environment conducive to holistic self-discovery and acceptance. The process demands sincere introspection and reflection, enabling individuals to acknowledge and come to terms with the inherent duality existing within their psyche. Moreover, this journey facilitates the bridging of polarities, fostering a greater sense of wholeness and balance within the individual. The assimilation of the anima/animus is instrumental in promoting an integrated and authentic sense of self, transcending conventional dichotomies and enabling the realization of a more comprehensive personal identity. Throughout this transformative process, individuals are encouraged to explore artistic and creative outlets as avenues for engaging with and expressing the myriad facets of their anima/animus. These endeavors serve as powerful mechanisms for nurturing a deeper connection with these aspects, thereby fostering a more profound comprehension of the complexities embedded within the psyche. Furthermore, engaging with the anima/animus necessitates a delicate dance between embracing these inner archetypes and acknowledging the potential conflicts that may arise. It involves managing the dichotomous nature of these elements, working towards their harmonious coexistence, and forging a cohesive internal narrative.

### Emergence of the Self

The journey through the stages of individuation ultimately leads to the emergence of the self, a complex process of discovering inner unity. At this crucial stage, individuals experience a deep sense of integration and wholeness as they transcend the fragmentation of their psyche. Through the reconciling of opposing forces and the assimilation of unconscious elements, the individual begins to recognize and embrace their authentic identity. This emergence signifies the culmination of the individuation process, marking a significant transformation in the individual's psychological development. As the self emerges, individuals become more attuned to their true nature, cultivating a heightened awareness of their unique strengths, values, and purpose. This newfound self-awareness empowers individuals to align with their genuine desires and aspirations, transcending societal expectations and external influences. With greater self-knowledge, individuals journey through life with clarity and conviction, making intentional choices that are congruent with their inner truth. The emergence of the self also fosters a profound sense of inner peace and harmony, as individuals find equilibrium amidst the complexities of their internal and external worlds. With this newfound internal coherence, individuals can engage authentically and meaningfully in their interpersonal relationships, fostering deeper connections and understanding with others. Furthermore, the discovery of inner unity paves the way for enhanced creativity and self-expression, as individuals access a rich wellspring of personal authenticity and originality. This creative unfolding allows individuals to contribute unique perspectives and innovations to the world, enriching not only their own lives but also the lives of those around them. Moreover, the emergence of the self is a continuous and dynamic process, inviting individuals to cultivate an ongoing relationship with their evolving identity. This continuous exploration and refinement engender a sense of resilience and adaptability, enabling individuals to face life's challenges with steadfastness and flexibility.

## The Role of Dreams and Symbols in Psychological Development

In the sphere of dreams, symbolic imagery often emerges as a representation of the unconscious content that is seeking integration into consciousness. Analyzing these symbols provides a bridge between conscious awareness and unconscious material. Through dream analysis, individuals can explore the depths of their psyche, uncover repressed emotions, and gain a deeper understanding of their inner conflicts and desires.

The archetypal symbolism present in dreams connects individuals to universal human experiences and emotions. These archetypes, such as the hero, the shadow, or the wise old man, resonate across cultures and epochs, carrying collective significance and influence. By recognizing and engaging with these archetypal symbols, individuals can tap into shared human narratives and transcend personal limitations, fostering integration and self-discovery.

Symbols are not limited to the dream world; they also manifest in waking life through various mediums like art, religion, and cultural rituals. For instance, religious symbols hold profound meaning and provide a framework for understanding existential questions and the mysteries of life. Similarly, artistic expression serves as a channel for unconscious material to manifest, allowing the individual to externalize and confront aspects of the self through creative endeavors.

Jung emphasized the importance of active imagination as a tool for engaging with symbols and archetypes. By actively dialoguing with these symbols through creative expression, individuals can gain insight into the unconscious forces shaping their behavior and perceptions. This process fosters introspection, personal growth, and the integration of disparate elements within the psyche.

The study of mythological narratives and folklore reveals recurring symbols and motifs that reflect fundamental aspects of human experience. These timeless stories and symbols offer wisdom and guidance, providing a rich tapestry for individuals to contextualize their own journeys towards individuation.

**Transformation Through Creativity and Expression**

Transformation through creativity and expression allows individuals to access and integrate unconscious material into conscious awareness. Creative endeavors such as art, music, writing, and other forms of expression provide a channel for exploring and giving form to the depths of the psyche. Carl Jung emphasized the significance of engaging with the creative impulse as a means of fostering psychological growth and self-realization. Through creative acts, individuals can unveil hidden aspects of their inner selves, confront unresolved conflicts, and make sense of their lived experiences. The act of creation becomes a bridge between the conscious and unconscious domains, facilitating the expression of archetypal themes and universal symbols that resonate with the collective unconscious. By engaging in creative processes, individuals can access symbolic representations of their personal and collective unconscious, initiating a transformative journey toward wholeness. Moreover, creativity offers a non-verbal mode of communication that transcends linguistic barriers, enabling individuals to articulate complex emotions and experiences that may otherwise elude conscious comprehension. This avenue of expression provides a safe space for exploring and integrating disowned or marginalized aspects of the self, promoting a sense of internal harmony and balance. Additionally, the act of creating can serve as a release from psychological tension, offering a cathartic outlet for emotional expression and processing. Furthermore, creative endeavors often entail a process of reimagining the world, allowing individuals to transcend conventional thought patterns and societal norms, thereby fostering innovative perspectives and novel solutions to inner conflicts. Beyond its personal impact, creative expression can also contribute to the enrichment of collective culture, serving as a source of inspiration and insight for others.

### Interplay of Personal Experiences and Collective Unconscious

Personal experiences are undeniably influential in shaping an individual's understanding of the world and themselves. However, Carl Jung postulated that personal experiences are not the only determinants of a person's psyche. The collective unconscious, as conceived by Jung, is a reservoir of primordial images and archetypes shared by all of humanity, influencing individuals on a subconscious level. The interplay between personal experiences and the collective unconscious is a complex dynamic that profoundly impacts an individual's psychological development. At the heart of this interplay is the concept of individuation, which entails integrating personal experiences with the universal symbols and motifs of the collective unconscious to achieve a sense of wholeness and self-realization. When examining the interplay of personal experiences and the collective unconscious, it becomes evident that both contribute to the formation of an individual's identity and psyche. Personal experiences, including early childhood memories, significant life events, and relationships, shape an individual's conscious narrative and emotional landscape. These experiences can evoke strong emotions, fears, desires, and motivations, influencing behavioral patterns and decision-making processes. Conversely, the collective unconscious exerts its influence through archetypal imagery and symbolic representations that resonate across cultures and time periods. Dreams, fantasies, myths, and religious motifs are manifestations of the collective unconscious and can imbue personal experiences with deeper meaning and significance. The process of individuation requires an individual to engage with both personal experiences and the collective unconscious in a way that acknowledges and integrates their respective influences. This often involves exploring one's personal narrative, identifying recurring themes and patterns, and recognizing underlying archetypal elements present in their experiences. By uncovering the symbolic content within personal experiences and relating them to universal archetypes, individuals can gain insight into their unconscious motivations, conflicts, and potential for growth. Moreover, the integration of personal experiences with archetypal symbolism can foster a greater understanding of oneself and cultivate a sense of connection to the broader human experience. Nonetheless, the interplay of personal experiences and the collective unconscious is not without challenges. Individuals may encounter resistance or skepticism when confronted with the idea of a collective unconscious or the significance of archetypal imagery in their lives. Furthermore, reconciling personal experiences with archetypal patterns can be a deeply introspective and at times confrontational process, requiring individuals to confront suppressed emotions, inner conflicts, and existential questions. Additionally, cultural and societal influences may shape the interpretation of personal experiences and archetypal symbolism, adding another layer of complexity to the interplay between the personal and the collective. Recognizing and addressing these challenges is essential for individuals undertaking the journey of individuation. In doing so, individuals can develop a more profound awareness of the interconnectedness of personal narratives with universal themes, facilitating a richer and more meaningful engagement with the process of psychological development.

## Challenges and Resistances in the Journey of Individuation

As individuals delve into their unconscious depths, they are often met with formidable obstacles that test their resolve and commitment to psychological development. One of the primary challenges encountered in the pursuit of individuation is the resistance of the ego. The ego, being the conscious part of the psyche, often resists the integration of unconscious contents as it strives to maintain familiar patterns and structures. This resistance may manifest as fear, anxiety, or a reluctance to embrace the unknown aspects of the self. Overcoming this innate resistance requires courage and a willingness to transcend the limitations of the ego's defenses.

The process of individuation may engender inner conflicts and emotional turmoil as individuals grapple with confronting repressed or disavowed aspects of their personality. Coming face-to-face with the shadow self and acknowledging its existence can evoke feelings of shame, guilt, and discomfort. These emotional struggles pose significant hurdles on the path to individuation, demanding introspection, self-compassion, and an acceptance of one's inherent complexity.

Another formidable challenge arises from societal and cultural influences that impose norms, expectations, and collective values onto individuals. These external pressures can hinder the authentic expression of individuality, leading to a sense of fragmentation and alienation. Overcoming these external influences demands a critical examination of societal conditioning and the cultivation of autonomy in aligning personal values with the evolving self.

The struggle with integrating conflicting archetypal forces, such as the anima and animus, presents a profound challenge in the individuation process. Balancing these inner polarities requires a harmonious reconciliation of opposing traits and qualities, necessitating a deep understanding of relational dynamics and gender identity within the psyche.

Facing existential dilemmas, confronting existential fears, and embracing existential questioning form additional dimensions of the challenges encountered along the path of individuation. These quintessential challenges compel individuals to confront the fundamental realities of existence, prompting a deep inquiry into the meaning and purpose of life, mortality, and the human condition.

## Consolidation and Continuity

As individuals traverse the path of individuation, they inevitably encounter various challenges and resistances that stand as formidable barriers to achieving wholeness. Overcoming these hurdles necessitates a process of consolidation and continuity, wherein the fragmented aspects of the psyche are integrated to culminate in a state of unity and completeness. This phase marks the culmination of the individuation journey, signifying the attainment of psychological equilibrium and harmony. Achieving wholeness involves the conscious assimilation of diverse psychological elements unearthed during the transformative process, leading to the harmonization of conflicting aspects of one's personality.

Central to the journey of achieving wholeness is the recognition and reconciliation of polarities within the self. This entails embracing and integrating the shadow side – the aspects of the unconscious that have been suppressed or denied. By acknowledging and assimilating these shadow elements, individuals foster inner balance and gain a deeper understanding of their true nature. Furthermore, achieving wholeness involves reconciling inner conflicts and tensions through a process of alignment, facilitating the emergence of a unified and authentic sense of self.

The pursuit of wholeness also encompasses the sustained development of one's individual identity, transcending societal expectations and norms. It demands the authentic expression of one's unique essence and the realization of one's deepest potential. In this context, individuals are compelled to acknowledge their intrinsic creative capacities and engage in endeavors that facilitate self-expression and personal evolution. Through creative pursuits such as art, music, writing, or other forms of expression, individuals embody their inner richness and continue the process of integration and wholeness.

Attaining wholeness involves the cultivation of a meaningful connection with the collective unconscious, accessing its vast wellspring of archetypal energies and symbols to further enrich the individual's inner landscape. This connection fosters a profound sense of belonging and interconnectedness, anchoring the individual in an expansive tapestry of shared human experiences. By acknowledging and honoring these universal archetypal patterns, individuals cultivate a deep sense of continuity and purpose, contributing to the realization of holistic and integrated existence.

Ultimately, the achievement of wholeness signifies the culmination of the individuation process, wherein individuals embrace their multifaceted nature and align with their authentic selves. The journey towards wholeness entails an ongoing commitment to introspection, reflection, and growth, culminating in the unification of disparate elements within the psyche. As individuals embrace their complexity and explore the intricacies of their inner world, they transcend fragmentation and emerge as whole, integrated beings, embodying the transformative power of individuation.

# INDIVIDUATION VS. PSYCHOSEXUAL DEVELOPMENT

## Fundamentals of Freud's Psychosexual Development

According to Sigmund Freud, the father of psychoanalysis, human personality is shaped by the interaction of biological drives and societal influences during distinct stages of psychosexual development. Freud postulated five sequential stages within his psychosexual theory: oral, anal, phallic, latent, and genital, each characterized by unique erogenous zones and developmental challenges. The oral stage, occurring from birth to 18 months, revolves around the baby's primary source of pleasure - the mouth. Freud emphasized the significance of feeding and weaning experiences in this stage, suggesting that unresolved conflicts may lead to fixation and subsequent personality traits. Subsequently, the anal stage, spanning from 18 months to 3 years, centers on toilet training and the child's control over bodily functions, with potential implications for self-control and orderliness in adulthood. The phallic stage, typically unfolding between ages 3 to 6, introduces the Oedipus and Electra complexes, pivotal in the formation of superego and gender identity. These early experiences profoundly influence the individual's relationships and outlook on life. Following the phallic stage, the latent phase ensues, manifesting from age 6 to puberty, characterized by the repression of sexual impulses and focus on intellectual and social pursuits. Finally, the genital stage encompasses puberty through adulthood, highlighting mature sexual interests and the capacity for intimate relationships. While Freud's psychosexual theory has garnered both acclaim and critique, its impact on psychological discourse is undeniable. Its emphasis on early childhood experiences and their enduring effects continues to inform therapeutic approaches and theoretical paradigms in contemporary psychology.

## Divergence in Conceptual Foundations

In analyzing the divergence in conceptual foundations between Jung's individuation and Freud's psychosexual development, it is imperative to delve into their dissimilar theoretical underpinnings. While Freud's psychoanalytic theory predominantly centers on the role of sexual instincts and the successive stages of libidinal development, Jung's individuation process emphasizes the integration and harmonization of the archetypal elements within the psyche. This fundamental contrast elucidates how the two theories diverge in their approach to understanding human development and psychological maturation. Freud's emphasis on the significance of early childhood experiences and the influence of libido in shaping personality traits stands in stark contrast to Jung's conception of individuation as a transformative and integrative process transcending the purely instinctual domain.

The concepts of the unconscious mind differ significantly in the two theories. Freud posits the presence of the id, ego, and superego as the structural components of the psyche, with the id being the reservoir of primal instincts driven by the pleasure principle. In contrast, Jung introduces the notion of the collective unconscious, housing universal symbolic representations called archetypes that exert a profound influence on an individual's psychological development. This distinction underscores the divergence in their conceptual foundations, illuminating the differing lenses through which they perceive the depths of the human psyche.

The interpretation of human motivation and behavior varies distinctly in both theories. Freud's theory emphasizes the pivotal role of the unconscious drives, particularly the sexual and aggressive instincts, in governing human actions. In contrast, Jung's individuation framework delineates a broader scope encompassing spiritual, creative, and transcendental aspects. This divergence in conceptual foundations inherently shapes the underlying premises of each theory, portraying distinct manifestations of human nature and the complexities inherent in the human psyche.

The philosophical orientations of Freud and Jung also contribute to the disparity in their conceptual frameworks. Freud's theory is deeply rooted in a deterministic perspective, attributing human behavior to predetermined biological factors and early experiences. Conversely, Jung's analytical psychology adopts a more teleological stance, emphasizing the aspirational nature of individuation towards self-realization and wholeness. This philosophical contrast not only accentuates the divergence in their conceptual foundations but also elucidates the differing viewpoints on the purpose and trajectory of human existence.

## Parallel Processes

Jung's concept of individuation emphasizes the integration of the conscious and unconscious aspects of the psyche, highlighting the transcendence of personal and collective archetypes as pivotal in the realization of selfhood. This deeply transformative process encompasses the journey towards wholeness and the actualization of one's unique potential. Conversely, Freud's psychosexual development theory revolves around the progression through distinct psychosexual stages, wherein the resolution of conflicts related to the erogenous zones determines an individual's personality structure.

Examining parallel processes necessitates a critical exploration of the role of self-awareness and the influence of early experiences on the construction of identity. Jung posits that the individuation process involves encountering and integrating the shadow, anima/animus, and other archetypal components, leading to a harmonious alignment of the conscious and unconscious. Conversely, Freud's emphasis on the impact of childhood experiences, particularly those pertaining to the satisfaction or frustration of basic instincts, underscores the formative influence of early relationships and the development of defense mechanisms.

The interplay between conscious and unconscious drives and desires plays a central role in both frameworks, albeit within differing contexts. Jung's focus on the transformation of unconscious contents and the manifestation of the Self echoes Freud's exploration of the id, ego, and superego as dynamic components shaping human behavior and personality. This parallels the network of internal conflicts and resolutions that pave the way for a cohesive sense of self in both theories.

The developmental trajectories articulated by Jung and Freud offer complementary perspectives on the multifaceted nature of identity formation and psychological growth. While Jung's individuation underscores the transcendent quest for self-realization and spiritual evolution, Freud's psychosexual development emphasizes the formative impact of early experiences and intrapsychic conflicts on the constitution of personality.

**Identity Formation and Psychological Growth**

The process of identity formation encompasses the complex interplay of individual experiences, social influences, and internal psychological dynamics. Jung's concept of individuation emphasizes the integration and harmonization of various aspects of the self, including the exploration of archetypes and the collective unconscious. This holistic approach focuses on achieving a balanced and authentic sense of self, transcending societal expectations and unconscious influences.

In contrast, Freud's psychosexual development theory highlights the significance of early childhood experiences, particularly the formation of personality through distinct stages related to erogenous zones. According to Freud, unresolved conflicts during these stages can lead to fixation and impact an individual's adult behaviors and perspectives.

The process of identity formation involves the construction of a coherent identity that accommodates the dynamic interplay between conscious and unconscious elements of the human psyche. It involves the exploration and eventual integration of various archetypal motifs that influence an individual's thoughts, emotions, and behaviors. Through this process, individuals endeavor to recognize and reconcile their own unique emotional and cognitive patterns, allowing for personal growth and adaptive responses to life's challenges.

Psychological growth is a multifaceted journey that encompasses the development of self-awareness, interpersonal relationships, and adaptation to life transitions. Jung emphasized the significance of psychological growth as a lifelong pursuit that leads to a more integrated and harmonious existence. Conversely, Freud's focus on the impact of early childhood experiences on later development underscores the enduring influence of formative years on an individual's identity and psychological functioning.

**Role of Archetypes versus Erogenous Zones**

Archetypes, as posited by Jung, are universal symbols and patterns that reside within the collective unconscious, shaping an individual's experiences and perceptions. These timeless and cross-cultural symbols play a pivotal role in the process of individuation, serving as templates for psychological integration and personal growth. In contrast, Freud's emphasis on erogenous zones highlights the significance of physical pleasure and the stages of psychosexual development during infancy and childhood as formative in an individual's personality. The preoccupation with the exploration and resolution of conflicts related to specific erogenous zones exemplifies Freud's psychoanalytic framework. However, while both frameworks acknowledge the importance of early experiences in shaping an individual's psyche, the conceptualization of these formative influences diverges significantly. Jung's emphasis on archetypes transcends individual developmental stages and underscores a more holistic and transcendent approach to understanding the human psyche, incorporating elements beyond basic physical needs and desires. Furthermore, the role of archetypes in Jungian psychology extends into the field of cultural myths, symbolism, and spiritual dimensions, providing a broader canvas for the individuation process, which contrasts sharply with the more exclusively psychosexual lens of Freudian theory. The influence of archetypes in manifesting universal themes and motifs across different cultures underpins Jung's assertion that individuation is not constrained by singular sexual or developmental experiences but encompasses a wider spectrum of human existence. Conversely, Freud's concentration on erogenous zones reflects a narrower focus on the resolution of libidinal energy and interpersonal dynamics rooted in early childhood experiences. This emphasis brings to light a contrasting perspective on the formative processes affecting psychological growth and integration.

**Integration vs. Fixation**

Integration, as proposed by Jung, pertains to the process of harmonizing the conscious and unconscious aspects of the self, leading to a balanced and individuated personality. Conversely, Freud's theory emphasizes the critical role of resolving conflicts at specific stages of psychosexual development to avoid fixation and ensure healthy adult functioning.

Examining the outcomes of these processes offers valuable insights into the complexities of human psychological growth. In Jungian psychology, successful integration results in a sense of wholeness and self-realization, where individuals develop a deep understanding of their unique identity and purpose. This holistic approach fosters adaptive coping mechanisms and resilience in the face of life's challenges, contributing to overall well-being.

On the other hand, Freud's emphasis on addressing conflicts within each psychosexual stage highlights the implications of unresolved fixations. Fixation at a particular stage can lead to enduring behavioral patterns and emotional tendencies, impacting relationships, decision-making, and self-perception. The consequences of fixation often manifest as neuroses or maladaptive behaviors, hindering individual fulfillment and impeding personal development.

The comparative outcomes of integration and fixation shed light on the varying degrees of agency and determinism within each theoretical framework. Jung's concept of individuation emphasizes the inherent capacity for self-discovery and growth, empowering individuals to actively engage in their psychological maturation and transformation. Alternatively, Freud's psychosexual development underscores the significance of early experiences and external influences in shaping adult personality, signaling a more deterministic perspective.

A nuanced examination of these comparative outcomes prompts consideration of the interplay between nature and nurture, autonomy and environmental impact, and the dynamic nature of human development. Furthermore, it fosters a deeper understanding of the multifaceted factors contributing to individual differences, drawing attention to the diverse pathways through which individuals journey through their psychological evolution.

### Theoretical Implications and Criticisms

One of the central areas of divergence between Freud and Jung lies in their contrasting views on the role of unconscious processes in shaping personality. Jung's emphasis on the collective unconscious and archetypes as pivotal forces in individuation stands in stark contrast to Freud's focus on the influence of early childhood experiences, particularly related to sexuality and the Oedipus complex. This fundamental difference has far-reaching implications for understanding human development and the nature of psychological transformation.

Critically evaluating these two frameworks also invites scrutiny regarding their applicability and universality across diverse cultural and social contexts. While both Jung and Freud operated within particular historical and cultural milieus, concerns have been raised about the extent to which their theories can be generalized beyond Western, individualistic societies. The potential ethnocentric bias of these theories necessitates a nuanced examination to discern the extent of their relevance in global multicultural settings.

The theoretical underpinnings and the resulting therapeutic approaches derived from these frameworks have not been immune to criticisms. Freud's psychoanalytic methods, with an overarching focus on uncovering repressed memories and resolving unresolved conflicts, have sparked debates about the potential retraumatization of individuals and the subjective nature of interpretation. On the other hand, Jung's concepts, though embracing a more holistic and spiritual dimension, have faced skepticism regarding their scientific rigor and empirical substantiation.

The criticisms extend to the practical implications of these theories in clinical settings and broader societal contexts. Questions abound about the gender biases inherent in Freud's constructs and the potential reinforcement of traditional gender roles. Similarly, Jung's archetype theory has been scrutinized for its potential to perpetuate essentialist notions about identity and limit the agency of individuals.

In conclusion, while the comparative analysis of Jung's individuation and Freud's psychosexual development illuminates crucial insights into the domains of personality formation and psychological growth, it also unveils a spectrum of theoretical implications and criticisms that demand conscientious reflection and refinement. Addressing these intricacies is integral to advancing a more inclusive and comprehensive understanding of human psychology.

## CRITIQUES AND COUNTERARGUMENTS

### Philosophical and Theoretical Objections

In the exploration of Jung's theory of individuation, it is crucial to consider the philosophical and theoretical objections that have been raised over time. One of the primary philosophical objections revolves around the subjective nature of Jungian concepts such as archetypes and the collective unconscious. Critics argue that these concepts are inherently abstract and lack empirical grounding, raising doubts about their validity within the framework of scientific inquiry. Additionally, the theoretical objections encompass concerns regarding the complexity and ambiguity of the individuation process. Some scholars contend that Jung's emphasis on the individual's journey towards self-realization may overlook the wider sociocultural dynamics and power structures that shape an individual's experiences. This raises fundamental questions about the universality and applicability of the theory across diverse contexts and societies. Moreover, from a theoretical standpoint, there are ongoing debates about the integration of spirituality and mysticism in Jungian psychology. Critics argue that the incorporation of spiritual elements blurs the boundaries between psychology and theology, potentially compromising the scientific rigor of the theory. Furthermore, philosophical objections extend to the potential deterministic undertones within the conceptualization of archetypes and the collective unconscious. Critics caution against reducing human behavior and experiences to predetermined patterns, emphasizing the need for a more nuanced understanding of individual agency and cultural influences.

### Empirical Challenges

The nature of individuation, with its focus on individual experiences, subjective perceptions, and personal growth, poses significant hurdles for empirical investigation. Traditional empirical methods often prioritize quantifiable and observable phenomena, which may not fully capture the intricacies of individuation. Additionally, the inherent subjectivity and internal nature of individuation make it challenging to develop standardized measurement tools that can accurately assess an individual's progress along this developmental path. Furthermore, the dynamic and nonlinear nature of individuation complicates the establishment of consistent measurement criteria or assessment frameworks. This non-linear progression and individual variation in the process further hinder attempts to formulate universally applicable measurement instruments. Moreover, ethical considerations surrounding the measurement of deeply personal and subjective experiences pose additional complexities. The potential intrusion into individuals' inner worlds raises questions about informed consent, privacy, and the potential impact of measurement processes on the very experiences they seek to capture. The development of comprehensive and sensitive measures for individuation requires interdisciplinary collaboration across psychology, anthropology, philosophy, and other relevant fields. By integrating diverse perspectives, researchers can strive to create multi-faceted assessment tools that encompass the interplay of cognitive, emotional, social, and cultural dimensions inherent in the process of individuation. Incorporating qualitative research methods, such as in-depth interviews, narrative analysis, and self-reported assessments, offers a promising approach to capturing the nuanced aspects of individuation beyond the traditional quantitative measurements. These qualitative approaches enable researchers to delve into the rich tapestry of personal narratives, cultural influences, and existential meanings that underpin individuation, contributing to a more holistic understanding of this transformative process. Additionally, advancements in technology, including virtual reality simulations and psychophysiological monitoring, present innovative avenues for examining individuation in real-time contexts and capturing subtle behavioral and physiological indicators of psychological growth. However, ethical considerations regarding the use of such advanced technologies in researching highly personal aspects of human experience necessitate careful reflection and oversight. Embracing the complexity and richness of individuation necessitates a nuanced and multifaceted approach to measurement, one that acknowledges the intrinsic subjectivity and diversity of individual journeys toward wholeness and self-realization.

## Cultural Relativism

Cultural relativism poses a significant quandary in the discourse surrounding the theory of individuation propounded by Carl Jung. It addresses the contentious issue of whether the process of individuation, as explicated by Jungian psychology, is universally applicable across diverse cultural contexts or whether it is inherently bound by the specificities and nuances of individual cultures. This debate is situated at the intersection of psychological theory, anthropology, and sociology, and it necessitates an in-depth exploration of the interplay between universal human experiences and culturally contingent practices and beliefs.

Proponents of universality argue that the fundamental elements of individuation, such as the realization of the self and the integration of unconscious material, are inherent to the human psyche irrespective of cultural diversity. They assert that the archetypal motifs and symbolic representations encountered in the individuation process transcend cultural boundaries, thereby endorsing a universalistic perspective. In contrast, advocates of cultural contextuality emphasize the influence of socio-cultural determinants on the processes and outcomes of individuation. They propose that the manifestations of individuation are shaped by cultural norms, values, and rituals, thereby highlighting the necessity of considering cultural specificity in the application of Jungian principles.

The discussion of cultural relativism within the framework of individuation extends beyond theoretical conjectures and delves into practical implications for clinical practice and cross-cultural psychology. It prompts an exploration of how therapeutic interventions based on the concept of individuation must be tailored to accommodate the diversity of cultural backgrounds and belief systems among individuals seeking psychological treatment.

Furthermore, it raises crucial ethical considerations regarding the imposition of universalized frameworks of psychological development in culturally distinct contexts, necessitating a nuanced understanding of the dialectics between universality and contextuality.

In addressing the conundrum of cultural relativism, it becomes imperative to engage in multifaceted dialogues that integrate perspectives from multicultural psychology, anthropological studies, and cognitive neuroscience. Such interdisciplinary engagements can provide valuable insights into the dynamic interactions between psychological processes and cultural influences, thereby enriching our comprehension of the complexities inherent in the theory of individuation. Through an examination of cultural relativism, we can address the paradoxes of universality and contextuality in the pursuit of a more inclusive and culturally responsive approach to individuation within the broader landscape of Jungian psychology.

## Psychological Legitimacy

The concept of psychological legitimacy within the framework of individuation has been a subject of heated debate among scholars, practitioners, and researchers in the field of psychology. This discourse revolves around the fundamental constructs and principles that underpin the theory of individuation as proposed by Carl Jung. One of the central debates pertains to the legitimacy of archetypes and the collective unconscious, which are integral components of Jung's theory. Critics argue that the existence and influence of universal symbols and patterns, as posited by the archetype hypothesis, lacks empirical evidence and scientific substantiation. Conversely, proponents emphasize the phenomenological and transpersonal experiences reported by individuals across different cultures, suggesting a shared reservoir of symbolic imagery and motifs. The contested nature of archetypes raises essential questions regarding the applicability and veracity of these constructs within contemporary psychological discourse. Moreover, the debate extends to the notion of the collective unconscious and its role in shaping individual experiences and expressions. Scholars advocate for exploring alternative explanations rooted in cultural, social, and cognitive psychology, while acknowledging the need for a more nuanced and integrated approach to understanding the psyche. Another focal point of contention revolves around the process of self-realization and psychic wholeness, central tenets of individuation. Critics question the transcendental aspects of the self and the transformative journey towards integration, positing that such concepts lack empirical grounding and solid theoretical foundation. In response, advocates highlight the subjective narratives of individuals who have undergone profound personal growth and individuation, emphasizing their lived experiences as compelling evidence of the transformative potential inherent in the individuation process. Furthermore, the debate about the legitimacy of the self as an organizing principle for psychological development underscores the intersection of existential, humanistic, and depth psychologies. It urges a reevaluation of the ontological and epistemological assumptions that underlie contemporary psychological paradigms, prompting a critical examination of the evolving discourses within the field.

### Interdisciplinary Rebuttals

A number of critics and skeptics have raised valid concerns regarding the psychological legitimacy of Jung's constructs, with some questioning their alignment with empirical findings in neuroscience. However, a compelling interdisciplinary rebuttal can be presented by examining the insights emerging from neuroscience that intersect with and support core aspects of Jung's theory of individuation.

Neuroscientific research has illuminated the workings of the brain, shedding light on mechanisms related to identity formation, emotional regulation, and self-integration—concepts central to Jungian individuation. The burgeoning field of neuroplasticity, for instance, has unveiled the brain's remarkable capacity for adaptive change and reorganization, offering neurobiological underpinnings for the transformative processes inherent in individuation. Moreover, the exploration of neural correlates of archetype activation and symbol processing provides intriguing parallels to Jung's elucidation of archetypal imagery and its psychological significance.

The investigation of neural networks associated with introspective and reflective processes aligns with Jung's emphasis on self-inquiry, introspection, and individuation as an inward journey toward self-awareness and integration. Studies on the default mode network, which underpins self-referential cognition and autobiographical memory, converge with Jung's conceptualization of the individuation process as an unfolding narrative of personal evolution and realization.

Beyond structural and functional neuroimaging, the field of psychopharmacology offers additional insights into the neurochemical foundations of psychological transformation and resilience, complementing Jung's emphasis on confronting the shadow and attaining psychological wholeness. The modulation of neurotransmitter systems implicated in mood regulation, such as serotonin and dopamine, raises intriguing implications for understanding the affective dimensions of individuation and the management of psychic conflicts.

In essence, while acknowledging the necessity for continued dialogue and synthesis between psychology, neuroscience, and related disciplines, the burgeoning convergence of neuroscientific evidence with fundamental tenets of Jung's theoretical framework provides compelling interdisciplinary rebuttals against criticisms of his theories' scientific validity. These interdisciplinary dialogues underscore the dynamic interplay between psychological concepts and their neural substrates, fostering a holistic perspective on human development and transformation.

**Comparative Critiques**

In the field of developmental psychology, numerous theories vie for preeminence alongside Jung's concept of individuation. One notable rival to Jung's individuation is Erik Erikson's psychosocial development stages, which emphasize the centrality of social influences and continuity of development across the lifespan. Contrasting with Jung's focus on the individual's internal journey, Erikson delineates distinct psychosocial crises that shape an individual's identity and interactions with society.

On the other hand, Jean Piaget's cognitive development theory presents a compelling counterpoint to Jung's framework. Piaget's emphasis on the role of cognition in shaping psychological growth and adaptive behaviors diverges from Jung's archetypal models and collective unconscious. While Jungian individuation underscores the integration of unconscious contents, Piaget's stages emphasize the progressive construction of schemas and mental structures. These differing perspectives warrant critical examination to elucidate the nuances and applicability of each approach.

Additionally, Lawrence Kohlberg's theory of moral development offers a contrasting lens through which to evaluate individuation. Where Jung's theory delves into the integration of archetypal symbols and personal myths, Kohlberg's sequential stages of moral reasoning prioritize ethical decision-making and universal principles. Understanding the interplay between moral development and individuation invites discussions on the complex interdependence of morality and personal growth.

Plus, it is essential to address Lev Vygotsky's sociocultural theory, emphasizing the interaction between culture and individual development. Vygotsky's focus on the role of social mediation and cultural tools in shaping cognitive processes challenges the predominantly internal perspective embedded within Jungian individuation. The juxtaposition of Vygotsky's framework with Jung's underscores the indispensable influence of external sociocultural factors on the individuation process, thereby enriching the discourse on human development.

## Influence of External Factors

One significant aspect that demands close examination is the influence of external factors, particularly societal and environmental influences, on the process of individuation. These external elements play a pivotal role in shaping an individual's psyche and molding their path toward wholeness and self-realization. Societal norms, cultural values, and environmental circumstances can significantly impact the individuation journey, posing both facilitative and inhibitory effects.

Societal and cultural norms imbue individuals with collective expectations, norms, and values that may either align with or conflict with their innate predispositions and personal growth trajectories. The ethos of society, including its attitudes towards conformity, collectivism, and individualism, can exert considerable influence on an individual's willingness to explore and integrate conflicting aspects of the self. Moreover, cultural constructs regarding gender roles, power dynamics, and societal hierarchies can profoundly shape an individual's understanding of themselves and their relationship with the world. These cultural imprints often intersect with the individuation process, potentially influencing the interpretation and integration of archetypal imagery and unconscious content.

Environmental factors such as socioeconomic status, geographical location, and access to resources also bear significance in the individuation process. Individuals from marginalized communities may encounter additional barriers and stressors that impede their pursuit of self-discovery and actualization. Conversely, those in more privileged positions may have increased opportunities for introspection, personal development, and therapeutic exploration. Furthermore, environmental factors encompassing familial dynamics, social support networks, and historical legacies can deeply impact one's psychological well-being and create varying degrees of receptivity to the individuation process.

Understanding the interplay between societal and environmental influences and the individuation journey is crucial for comprehending the complexities inherent in this transformative process. By acknowledging the multifaceted nature of external influences, we can develop more nuanced approaches to supporting and guiding the process of individuation. Incorporating an awareness of societal and environmental dynamics into therapeutic practices and personal development endeavors fosters a more inclusive, holistic, and empathetic approach to individuation.

**Misinterpretations and Misapplications**

Misinterpretations and misapplications of Jung's theory often arise from a lack of comprehensive understanding or oversimplification of the complex concepts underlying individuation. One common misinterpretation revolves around the oversimplification of archetypes as mere stereotypes or universal templates, neglecting their dynamic and multifaceted nature as symbolic representations of deep-seated psychological patterns and potentialities.

Misapplications of Jungian concepts can lead to the adoption of rigid, deterministic viewpoints that disregard the fluid and evolving nature of individuation. For instance, the concept of the 'shadow' may be misapplied to justify negative behaviors or traits without acknowledging the imperative need for conscious integration and reconciliation. Such misinterpretations not only distort the essence of individuation but also hinder its potential transformative power.

To address these misinterpretations and misapplications, it is crucial to emphasize the nuanced and context-sensitive nature of Jung's theories. This involves promoting a deeper grasp of the symbolic and metaphorical aspects of his concepts, steering away from literal and reductionist interpretations. Additionally, fostering an open dialogue and critical discourse within scholarly communities can serve as a platform for addressing misinterpretations and misapplications. By inviting diverse perspectives and encouraging introspective examination, the field can progress beyond surface-level understanding towards a more profound comprehension of individuation.

Practitioners and scholars should actively engage in self-reflection and self-critique to identify and rectify potential instances of misinterpretation and misapplication within their own professional practices. This requires a continual dedication to refining one's understanding of Jungian psychology and remaining receptive to evolving interpretations and insights. Moreover, mentorship and collaborative forums can offer guidance and correction, enabling individuals to manage the complexities of individuation with greater precision and integrity.

# METHODOLOGIES IN RESEARCH ON INDIVIDUATION

## Historical Overview of Research Approaches in Individuation

The early stages of research into individuation predominantly revolved around qualitative inquiries, driven by the desire to comprehend the symbolic and transformative nature of individuation experiences. Scholars sought to capture the nuances of individuals' journeys toward self-realization through in-depth interviews, rich narratives, and thematic analysis of personal accounts. These qualitative investigations laid the foundation for uncovering the archetypal motifs and mythological patterns that underpin the individuation process.

As the field of psychology continued to embrace empirical rigor, a shift toward quantitative research methodologies emerged in the study of individuation. Researchers endeavored to quantify aspects of the individuation process, employing instruments such as psychometric scales and standardized assessments to measure and analyze psychological transformation. This transition allowed for the systematic exploration of developmental markers, cognitive shifts, and personality dynamics associated with individuation, fostering a deeper understanding of its psychological dimensions.

The interdisciplinary nature of individuation research became increasingly apparent as scholars sought to integrate insights from fields such as anthropology, mythology, and religious studies. By delving into cultural manifestations of individuation and comparative analyses of diverse narratives, researchers elucidated the universality of individuation themes across different contexts, expanding the contextual framework for comprehending this fundamental process.

The evolution of research methodologies in the study of individuation showcases a continual endeavor to refine and synthesize diverse approaches, culminating in mixed-methods strategies that synergistically harness the strengths of both qualitative and quantitative paradigms. This integrative approach enables researchers to triangulate findings, validate interpretations, and enrich the depth of understanding pertaining to the multifaceted facets of individuation.

## Qualitative Methods

Utilizing qualitative methodologies allows us to capture the rich, context-bound experiences of individuals undergoing their unique journey towards self-realization. On the other hand, by closely examining the life stories, dreams, and symbolic manifestations of individuals, we can elucidate the archetypal motifs and unconscious dynamics at play within the psyche.

Narrative analysis further enriches the qualitative approach by identifying recurring themes, symbols, and patterns within the narratives of individuals undergoing individuation. Through systematic analysis of these narratives, we can uncover the evolving relationships with archetypal figures, confrontations with shadow aspects, and the navigation of the collective unconscious. The interpretive nature of narrative analysis enables the identification of transformative moments, pivotal conflicts, and the evolving sense of self within the individual's story.

Qualitative methodologies offer a holistic perspective, emphasizing the subjective dimensions of individuation that quantitative approaches may overlook. They allow for a nuanced exploration of the complexities inherent in the individuation process, recognizing the unique interplay between personal experiences and archetypal manifestations.

## Quantitative Approaches

Quantitative research methodologies in the study of individuation encompass a diverse range of strategies aimed at systematically measuring and analyzing observable phenomena related to Jungian concepts.

Surveys are instrumental tools utilized to gather structured information from participants, portraying their perspectives, attitudes, and behaviors in relation to individuation processes. By designing survey questionnaires grounded in Jungian theoretical constructs, researchers can acquire valuable insights into individual experiences of archetypal manifestations, symbolic imagery, and transformative journeys. Additionally, survey-based inquiries may probe into the manifestation of collective unconscious elements within the personal psyche, shedding light on the broader implications of individuation in the context of cultural and societal influences.

The utilization of scales serves as an effective means to quantitatively assess psychological attributes and tendencies associated with individuation. Psychometric scales tailored to measure factors such as archetype activation, ego integration, and symbolic engagement provide researchers with standardized metrics for evaluating the intensity and frequency of individuation-related phenomena. Through the administration of these scales, investigators obtain numerical data allowing for comparative analyses, trend identification, and correlation assessments, thus contributing to the establishment of empirical foundations for Jungian psychology.

Statistical interpretations form an integral component of quantitative approaches, enabling researchers to analyze and interpret numerical data derived from surveys, scales, and other quantitative instruments. Descriptive statistics offer insights into the central tendencies, distributions, and variations present within the collected data, facilitating the articulation of patterns and trends relevant to individuation dynamics. Moreover, inferential statistics empower researchers to draw broader conclusions and make substantive inferences regarding the relationships between various dimensions of individuation, thereby elucidating the underlying mechanisms of psychic transformation and transcendence.

## Mixed-Methods Strategies

Mixed-methods approaches have gained prominence in the field of Jungian psychology. By combining the strengths of both qualitative and quantitative methods, we can overcome the limitations inherent in each approach, leading to a more holistic examination of individuation processes.

Qualitative inquiries provide the depth and richness necessary to explore the subjective experiences and nuanced narratives of individuals undergoing the process of individuation. Through techniques such as in-depth interviews, thematic analysis, and phenomenological investigations, we can gain insights into the archetypal patterns and symbolic meanings that shape an individual's journey towards self-realization. These qualitative findings serve as the foundation for understanding the inner world of the psyche, capturing the intricacies of personal transformation.

On the other hand, quantitative methodologies offer the advantages of generalizability, rigor, and statistical validation. Surveys, psychometric scales, and experimental designs enable researchers to quantify and measure various dimensions of individuation, allowing for systematic comparisons and empirical validations across diverse populations. By analyzing large datasets and employing inferential statistics, quantitative studies contribute to establishing empirical evidence and identifying overarching trends within the individuation process.

The integration of qualitative and quantitative data through mixed-methods research provides a complementary and synergistic approach, yielding a more comprehensive understanding of individuation. By triangulating findings from different sources, we can corroborate their interpretations, mitigate biases, and construct a more robust narrative of the individuation phenomenon. Moreover, the convergence of qualitative narratives with quantitative measurements allows for a multi-faceted portrayal of the complexities inherent in the process of becoming whole.

Key considerations in employing mixed-methods strategies include the systematic integration of qualitative and quantitative data, ensuring methodological coherence, and attending to potential contradictions or divergent insights that may arise from the different approaches. Additionally, the ethical implications of merging various methodologies should be carefully addressed, prioritizing participant confidentiality, informed consent, and ethical conduct throughout the research process.

## Pioneering Research on Archetypes and Mythological Patterns

In the context of Jungian psychology, pioneering research on archetypes and mythological patterns has been instrumental in shaping our understanding of the collective unconscious and its symbolic manifestations. This area of study delves into the universal symbols and motifs that permeate human experiences across cultures and epochs. Scholars and researchers have endeavored to identify and analyze these archetypal images and narratives, drawing from diverse sources such as folklore, religion, literature, and art. Through meticulous exploration, these investigators seek to unearth the underlying psychological significance and pervasive influence of archetypes in shaping individual and collective psyches. Rather than dismissing mythology and symbolism as mere relics of the past, contemporary scholars have recognized their enduring relevance in elucidating human nature and the dynamics of the psyche.

The development of this field can be traced back to the groundbreaking works of early psychologists and mythologists who delved into the rich tapestry of symbolic imagery present in ancient myths and cultural narratives. An integral aspect of this research involves the identification and categorization of archetypal motifs that recur across different cultures, often exhibiting striking similarities despite varying historical and geographical contexts. The comparative approach adopted by scholars illuminates the profound resonance of archetypes, transcending temporal and spatial boundaries to communicate fundamental aspects of the human experience.

Modern advancements in fields such as neuroscience, anthropology, and cognitive science have provided novel insights into the symbolic processes underlying archetypal representations. Interdisciplinary collaborations have propelled the study of archetypes beyond the confines of traditional psychological inquiry, fostering a more comprehensive understanding of the interplay between mythological motifs and the human psyche. Cutting-edge techniques in neuroimaging and cognitive analysis offer promising avenues for unraveling the neurobiological underpinnings of archetypal activation and representation, shedding light on the mechanisms through which these universal symbols are integrated into the fabric of human cognition.

As this area of research continues to evolve, it holds immense potential for enriching not only the theoretical foundations of Jungian psychology but also for informing practical applications in therapy, education, and creative endeavors. By fathoming the depths of archetypal imagery and mythological patterns, scholars and we are poised to unlock new perspectives on human consciousness and the transformative power of symbolism in personal and collective growth.

### Interdisciplinary Connections

By integrating insights from various scientific domains, we can elucidate the intricacies of individuation and its implications across diverse contexts. One prominent area of interdisciplinary collaboration lies in the intersection of psychology with anthropology, where the exploration of cultural myths and rituals provides invaluable perspectives on archetypal motifs and their collective significance. Through comparative analysis of cross-cultural mythological narratives, psychologists gain insights into the universal underpinnings of individuation and its relevance within differing societal frameworks. Moreover, collaborations with neuroscience offer compelling avenues for investigating the neural correlates of individuation processes, delving into the interplay between psychological experiences and brain functionalities. Understanding how neurological mechanisms intertwine with psychological transformations enriches our comprehension of individuation from a holistic perspective. Additionally, linking psychology with sociology opens up new dimensions in comprehending the societal implications of individuation, shedding light on how individual transformation influences broader social structures and vice versa. Such multidisciplinary approaches not only enhance the depth of research on individuation but also pave the way for innovative methodologies and theoretical advancements. Beyond traditional disciplinary boundaries, these integrative endeavors foster a richer and more comprehensive understanding of the multifaceted nature of individuation.

## Ethical Considerations in Conducting Individuation Research

Given the deeply personal and transformative nature of the individuation process, researchers must uphold the highest standards of ethical conduct to protect the well-being and privacy of participants. One fundamental ethical consideration lies in informed consent, whereby participants are provided with comprehensive information about the research goals, procedures, potential risks, and their rights to confidentiality and withdrawal from the study at any time. In the context of researching individuation, individuals may be delving into profound aspects of their psyche, making it imperative for researchers to prioritize the well-being and autonomy of the participants. Additionally, ensuring the confidentiality and anonymity of participants is crucial to maintain their trust and safeguard sensitive personal disclosures. Researchers must establish secure data management protocols to protect the privacy of participants and responsibly handle any identifiable information gathered during the study. Furthermore, respecting cultural diversity and sensitivity when engaging with diverse populations in the research process is vital. This involves acknowledging and accommodating varying cultural perspectives, beliefs, and practices related to individuation, as well as being mindful of potential power differentials that may influence the dynamics of the research interaction. Additionally, ethical considerations extend to the dissemination of research findings, where authors must strive for accuracy, transparency, and responsible representation of the data, thereby avoiding sensationalism or distortion of results. Maintaining the integrity of the research process is also paramount, requiring researchers to critically self-reflect on their own biases and assumptions, and disclose any potential conflicts of interest that may impact the objectivity of the study. Lastly, ethical considerations in conducting individuation research demand ongoing vigilance towards the potential impact of the research on both individual participants and the broader community. This necessitates a commitment to assessing and mitigating any potential psychological or emotional distress that may arise as a result of participation in the study, as well as advocating for the responsible application of research findings in clinical and non-clinical settings. Striving to uphold the highest ethical standards in the pursuit of understanding and elucidating the complexities of individuation ensures the integrity and credibility of the research, while honoring the well-being and agency of those involved in the research process.

### Challenges in Empirical Investigation of Jungian Concepts

Empirical investigation of Jungian concepts poses several challenges stemming from the inherent nature of these concepts and their manifestation within the sphere of human consciousness. One primary challenge lies in the elusive and subjective nature of archetypes and the collective unconscious. Unlike observable and quantifiable phenomena, such as physical attributes or external behaviors, archetypes exist as universal symbols deeply embedded within the psyche, making their empirical study inherently complex.

The very essence of individuation, characterized by a deeply personal and transformative inner journey, presents challenges regarding standardization and measurement. Given that individuation is unique to each individual and manifests through diverse psychological processes, establishing standardized research parameters becomes inherently problematic.

Another significant challenge lies in the interplay between conscious and unconscious elements within the psyche. Jung's emphasis on the integration of the shadow and anima/animus archetypes underscores the dynamics involved in studying these phenomena empirically. Accessing and interpreting unconscious material presents methodological hurdles, as traditional research approaches often struggle to capture the nuances of the unconscious psyche.

The interdisciplinary nature of Jungian concepts necessitates an intersectional understanding that integrates psychology, mythology, philosophy, and spirituality. This complexity demands researchers to employ multidimensional approaches, requiring a comprehensive knowledge base across various domains.

Additionally, the historical context and cultural variations surrounding archetypes present challenges in conducting cross-cultural studies. Understanding how archetypes manifest differently within diverse cultural frameworks requires sensitivity to nuances and in-depth cultural understanding, posing further methodological complexities.

The reliance on introspective and self-reported data also introduces challenges, as individuals may struggle to articulate and verbalize profound and symbolic experiences related to individuation. This poses limitations on the reliability and validity of data collected, making it challenging to draw definitive empirical conclusions.

## Future Directions and Innovations in Methodological Approaches

As the field of Jungian psychology continues to evolve, it is imperative to anticipate the future directions and potential innovations in methodological approaches for researching individuation. One promising area of advancement lies in the integration of advanced technology, such as neuroimaging and physiological measures, to gain deeper insights into the neural correlates of archetypal experiences and individuation processes. This interdisciplinary collaboration between psychologists, neuroscientists, and technologists holds great promise for elucidating the biological underpinnings of Jungian concepts.

The advent of big data analytics offers an opportunity to explore large datasets to identify patterns and associations related to individuation. By harnessing computational power and sophisticated algorithms, researchers can delve into complex phenomena, such as synchronicities and meaningful coincidences, to uncover underlying principles that may inform the understanding of individuation.

Another constructive trajectory involves a renewed emphasis on cross-cultural studies and diverse global perspectives in researching individuation. By engaging with indigenous knowledge systems, spiritual traditions, and wisdom teachings from various cultural contexts, scholars can enrich the understanding of individuation as a universal process while respecting its culturally bound manifestations. This approach not only offers a broader ontological framework but also promotes inclusivity and diversity in the field.

The incorporation of longitudinal research designs presents a compelling avenue for tracing the dynamic trajectory of individuation over extended periods. Longitudinal studies can capture the nuances of individual transformation, shedding light on the ebbs and flows, as well as the enduring impact of the individuation process across the lifespan. By integrating qualitative narratives with quantitative measurements, researchers can paint a comprehensive picture of the multifaceted nature of individuation.

In addition, the burgeoning field of positive psychology provides a fertile ground for exploring the applications of Jungian individuation in fostering human flourishing and optimal functioning. By investigating the links between individuation, resilience, and well-being, researchers can uncover pathways for promoting psychological thriving and nurturing the realization of one's authentic self. This integrative approach aligns with the increasingly holistic orientation of contemporary psychology.

Lastly, embracing a reflexive and participatory stance in research methodologies by actively involving individuals undergoing the individuation process can yield profound insights. Empowering participants to co-create knowledge and offer experiential perspectives can deepen the authenticity and relevance of research findings, thereby bridging the gap between academic inquiry and lived realities.

# CONTEMPORARY APPLICATIONS AND IMPLICATIONS

## Individuation in Modern Therapy - Techniques and Practices

The integration of individuation principles into therapy revolves around the idea of guiding individuals through a transformative journey towards self-realization and psychological wholeness. Therapists often employ various methods to facilitate individuation, including dream analysis, active imagination, and exploring the symbolism of archetypes within the client's psyche. These techniques aim to uncover unconscious patterns, conflicts, and repressed aspects of the self, ultimately fostering greater self-awareness and growth. Furthermore, therapists embrace an empathetic, non-judgmental stance, providing a safe space for clients to delve into the depths of their psyche and confront unresolved issues. Cultivating a supportive therapeutic relationship is foundational in guiding individuals through the individuation process, encouraging them to manage the complexities of their inner world with courage and introspection. Additionally, therapists incorporate mindfulness-based interventions and holistic approaches to help individuals establish a deeper connection with their authentic self. By emphasizing the significance of integrating the conscious and unconscious aspects of the psyche, therapy becomes a transformative journey that enables individuals to achieve a sense of personal meaning and purpose. Moreover, modern therapeutic applications of individuation extend beyond traditional counseling sessions, encompassing group therapy, expressive arts therapies, and somatic experiencing to address the multidimensional nature of the individuation process. These diverse modalities aim to engage individuals on physical, emotional, mental, and spiritual levels, fostering a comprehensive approach to healing and self-discovery. Ultimately, the incorporation of individuation in modern therapy reflects a deep commitment to facilitating individuals' journeys towards achieving psychological integration, self-actualization, and a harmonious alignment with their inner potential.

## Personal Growth - The Role of Individuation in Self-Actualization

Self-actualization, a concept introduced by humanistic psychologist Abraham Maslow, represents the pinnacle of personal development and fulfillment. In the context of Jungian psychology, the process of individuation plays a pivotal role in facilitating an individual's journey towards self-actualization. At its core, individuation serves as a catalyst for individuals to become more self-aware, authentic, and aligned with their inner values and purpose. Through the process of individuation, individuals gain a deeper understanding of their unique psychological makeup, acknowledging both their strengths and vulnerabilities. This heightened self-awareness becomes the cornerstone for fostering personal growth and unlocking latent potentials. Moreover, the integration of archetypal energies and the exploration of the collective unconscious contribute to expanding one's consciousness and broadening their perspective on life. As individuals manage the complexities of their inner world, they begin to recognize and embrace their true selves, transcending societal expectations and external influences. Consequently, this process instills a sense of genuine authenticity and congruence within individuals, enabling them to lead lives that are more in alignment with their inherent nature. Furthermore, the pursuit of self-actualization through individuation involves a profound quest for meaning and purpose. By exploring the depths of their psyche and confronting existential dilemmas, individuals are empowered to uncover their unique calling and contribute meaningfully to the world. This transformative journey fosters a deep sense of fulfillment and allows individuals to live lives that are rich in significance and legacy. As such, it is evident that the principles of individuation hold profound implications for personal growth, paving the way for individuals to embark on a transformative odyssey towards self-actualization. In essence, the convergence of individuation and self-actualization represents the apotheosis of human development, signaling the realization of one's highest potential and the attainment of profound inner harmony.

## Educational Frameworks - Integrating Jungian Concepts

In the field of education, the integration of Jungian concepts offers a profound approach to understanding and nurturing the holistic development of individuals. Educational frameworks that incorporate Jungian psychology recognize the significance of the inner journey in the process of learning and personal growth. By delving into the depths of the psyche and acknowledging the existence of archetypes and the collective unconscious, educators can create an environment that fosters self-discovery and introspection. This approach goes beyond traditional pedagogy to embrace the multifaceted nature of human experience.

One key aspect of integrating Jungian concepts in education involves recognizing the diverse ways in which individuals perceive and process information. By acknowledging the influence of archetypal patterns on cognition and learning styles, educators can tailor their instructional methods to accommodate varying psychological dispositions. This inclusive approach promotes a more enriching and effective educational experience, allowing students to engage with the material in a manner that aligns with their innate psychological tendencies. By doing so, educators can empower students to embrace their individuality and unique mode of experiencing the world.

Educational frameworks rooted in Jungian psychology emphasize the cultivation of self-awareness and emotional intelligence as integral components of academic and personal development. Through initiatives such as reflective practices, mindfulness exercises, and the exploration of symbolism in literature and art, students are encouraged to embark on their own paths of individuation. By engaging with the depths of their inner worlds, individuals can develop a deeper understanding of themselves and others, leading to greater empathy, tolerance, and open-mindedness. These qualities not only enrich the educational experience but also prepare individuals to manage the complexities of the contemporary world with wisdom and resilience.

The integration of Jungian concepts in education extends beyond the individual to encompass the communal aspect of learning. By acknowledging the presence of collective unconscious dynamics within groups and communities, educational frameworks can promote collaboration, dialogue, and the appreciation of diverse perspectives. This approach nurtures a sense of interconnectedness and shared humanity, fostering an environment where mutual respect, cooperation, and constructive communication thrive. By creating such a milieu, educators contribute to the emergence of socially conscious and empathetic individuals who are poised to positively impact the larger society.

As educational institutions continue to evolve, the integration of Jungian concepts presents an opportunity to reimagine the purpose and potential of learning. By embracing the richness of the human psyche, educational frameworks can become transformative spaces that honor the process of individuation and empower individuals to realize their full potential.

## Organizational Development - Leadership through Individuation

Within the framework of Jungian psychology, the concept of individuation offers unique insights into enhancing leadership capabilities and fostering a harmonious organizational culture that values personal development and self-awareness. By integrating Jungian concepts into leadership development programs, organizations can cultivate leaders who are more attuned to their individual potential, adept at leveraging their strengths, and empathetic in their approach to guiding teams through challenges and opportunities.

At the heart of enhancing leadership through individuation lies the idea of embracing the shadow – acknowledging and integrating the darker aspects of the psyche that are often ignored or repressed. Leaders who embark on this introspective journey gain a deeper understanding of their own complexities, allowing them to relate more authentically to their team members and stakeholders. This self-awareness becomes a guiding force in decision-making, enabling leaders to discern their motives, biases, and unconscious influences, thereby fostering a more inclusive and compassionate leadership style.

The process of individuation equips leaders with the tools to recognize and transcend collective unconscious patterns within the organizational context. By deciphering archetypal dynamics at play and understanding how they shape group behavior, leaders can skillfully manage conflicts, inspire unity, and foster a culture of resilience and adaptability. Through this heightened awareness, leaders can facilitate constructive dialogue, co-create empowering narratives, and instill a sense of purpose that aligns with the organization's core values and mission.

Individuation also empowers leaders to embrace complexity and paradox, essential attributes in today's rapidly evolving business landscape. By engaging with their own inner conflicts and integrating opposing aspects of their personalities, leaders become more adept at managing ambiguity and leading with authenticity amidst uncertainty. This capacity for holding paradoxes extends to decision-making, where leaders can consider diverse perspectives and reconcile seemingly contradictory priorities, fostering an environment that embraces diversity of thought and encourages innovation.

## Cross-Cultural Perspectives on Individuation

In considering the cross-cultural perspectives on individuation, it is essential to recognize that while Jungian psychology has its roots in Western thought, its principles resonate with universal aspects of the human experience. Exploring how individuation manifests in various cultural contexts provides valuable insights into the collective unconscious, archetypal symbolism, and the journey towards self-realization.

One of the fundamental aspects of cross-cultural perspectives on individuation involves acknowledging the diversity of symbols, myths, and traditions that shape individual and collective identities. Different cultures exhibit unique mythological narratives and symbolic expressions that influence the processes of individuation within their respective communities. From African tribal traditions to Eastern philosophical systems, the exploration of archetypes and the collective unconscious unveils interconnected patterns that underpin humanity's quest for wholeness and integration.

Examining the cultural implications of individuation offers an opportunity to address the challenges of globalization and intercultural communication. In today's interconnected world, individuals from distinct cultural backgrounds encounter a myriad of influences that significantly impact their individuation journey. By embracing cross-cultural perspectives on individuation, we can foster greater understanding, empathy, and harmony amidst cultural diversity, paving the way for a more inclusive and integrated global society.

The study of cross-cultural perspectives on individuation sheds light on the role of societal norms, beliefs, and value systems in shaping individual identity and psychological development. Understanding how different cultures approach concepts such as the shadow, anima/animus, and persona provides a nuanced comprehension of human behaviors and attitudes within specific cultural milieus. By recognizing the cultural nuances of individuation, mental health professionals, educators, and policymakers can tailor interventions and initiatives that honor diverse cultural expressions of personal growth and transformation.

### Technology and Individuation

As modern society continues to embrace technological advancements, the intersection of technology and individuation becomes increasingly relevant. The digital age presents both challenges and opportunities for individuals seeking to undergo the process of individuation. The widespread use of technology can potentially hinder the individuation journey by promoting distraction, instant gratification, and superficial connections. Moreover, the constant bombardment of digital information may impede introspection and self-reflection, crucial components of the individuation process. On the other hand, technology also provides unprecedented opportunities for self-discovery and personal growth. Digital platforms offer access to a wealth of knowledge, diverse perspectives, and virtual communities where individuals can explore and express their authentic selves. Moreover, digital tools such as meditation apps, self-help resources, and virtual therapy sessions facilitate the integration of psychological insights and practices into everyday life. The use of wearable technology for tracking physical and mental well-being also aligns with the holistic approach of individuation, emphasizing the importance of mind-body connection. Furthermore, the digital sphere has become a space for creative expression and artistic exploration, enabling individuals to integrate their inner experiences and unconscious material into tangible forms through mediums such as digital art, virtual reality, and multimedia storytelling. However, it is crucial to traverse the digital landscape mindfully in the pursuit of individuation. Balancing screen time with periods of solitude, nature immersion, and face-to-face interactions is essential for maintaining a connection with the deeper aspects of one's psyche. Additionally, critical awareness of the impact of social media, online consumerism, and algorithmic influence on personal identity is paramount in harnessing the positive potential of technology for individuation. Overall, the digital age presents a complex and evolving context for individuation, requiring individuals to manage the challenges and leverage the opportunities offered by technology in their quest for self-discovery and wholeness.

## Art and Expression - Creative Manifestations of the Individuation Process

Art serves as a powerful vehicle for self-exploration, providing individuals with unique opportunities to externalize internal experiences, thoughts, and emotions. The process of engaging in artistic endeavors can mirror the stages of individuation described by Jung, as individuals confront their unconscious and integrate fragmented aspects of the self. Through various forms of expression such as painting, sculpture, music, dance, literature, and more, individuals embark on a journey of self-discovery and transformation, echoing the archetypal themes pervasive in the collective unconscious. Artists often tap into universal symbols and myths, resonating with audiences on a subconscious level and exemplifying the interconnectedness of human experience.

Art therapy, in particular, has emerged as a therapeutic modality that harnesses the creative process to facilitate individuation. Individuals engage in guided artistic activities, allowing them to bypass traditional verbal communication and access deeper layers of the psyche. As they explore their creations within a supportive and reflective environment, individuals gain insight into their inner world, fostering personal growth and integration. Artistic expression becomes a gateway for individuals to express and embody their evolving sense of identity, enabling them to reconcile conflicting elements within themselves and transcend limitations.

The act of creating art can serve as a transformative and healing force, catalyzing the individuation process. By externalizing internal struggles and conflicts through artistic mediums, individuals can reframe their narratives, release emotional burdens, and unveil unrecognized potential. The very act of creation embodies the alchemical process of transmuting inner turmoil into expressions of beauty, resilience, and authenticity. It is through this transcendent process that individuals come to acknowledge and embrace the complexities of their psyche, ultimately fostering wholeness and self-realization.

Beyond individual transformation, art and expression also hold the power to effect societal and cultural change. Creativity serves as a catalyst for collective introspection, inspiring dialogue and challenging established norms. Through art, individuals can communicate shared experiences, provoke critical reflection, and advocate for social justice. Thus, the creative manifestations of individuation extend beyond personal development, shaping the broader narrative of human existence and contributing to the evolution of consciousness.

## Societal Impacts - Collective Unconscious and Social Change

The societal impacts of individuation, particularly concerning the collective unconscious and social change, represent a fascinating intersection of Jungian psychology and broader cultural dynamics. At the heart of this discussion is the concept of the collective unconscious, a reservoir of shared human experiences, symbols, and archetypes that transcends individual consciousness and influences societal behavior and evolution. Understanding the role of the collective unconscious in shaping social norms, values, and narratives is essential for exploring the potential for positive social change.

When we examine the collective unconscious through the lens of individuation, we uncover the deep-seated patterns and symbolic representations that underpin societal structures and institutions. By recognizing and engaging with these underlying archetypal forces, individuals and communities can promote greater awareness and transformation within the collective psyche. This process can lead to shifts in societal attitudes, beliefs, and behaviors, ultimately contributing to meaningful and sustainable social change.

One significant example of the collective unconscious influencing social change can be observed in movements aimed at addressing systemic injustices and inequalities. These movements often tap into archetypal motifs and symbols that resonate with a broad segment of the population, catalyzing collective action and solidarity. Moreover, by bringing unconscious elements into conscious awareness, individuals and groups engaging in these movements can challenge established power dynamics and advocate for more equitable and just societal structures.

The understanding of the collective unconscious and its influence on social change has profound implications for fields such as governance, policy-making, and conflict resolution. By acknowledging the archetypal underpinnings of societal narratives and dynamics, leaders and decision-makers can appreciate the deeper psychological currents at play within their communities. This awareness can inform more empathetic and inclusive approaches to governance, fostering environments that prioritize collaboration, compassion, and sustainable progress.

In essence, the exploration of the societal impacts of the collective unconscious and individuation opens avenues for transformative social dialogue and action. It invites us to consider how a deeper understanding of our shared psychological heritage can propel us towards a more harmonious, equitable, and empathetic society. As we manage the complexities of contemporary challenges, embracing the potential of individuation to catalyze positive social change may serve as an essential cornerstone for building a more integrated and enlightened global community.

### Emerging Trends and Innovations

In considering the trajectory of Jungian psychology and the concept of individuation, it is pertinent to delve into the future landscape and explore the emerging trends and innovations that are shaping the field. As society continues to undergo rapid transformations driven by technological advancements, globalization, and an evolving socio-cultural fabric, the implications for individuation theory and its practical applications become increasingly significant.

A key area of interest in the future landscape of individuation lies in the intersection of psychology and technology. With the proliferation of digital platforms, artificial intelligence, and virtual reality, there is a growing opportunity to explore innovative approaches to facilitate individuation processes. From utilizing immersive digital experiences to simulate archetypal encounters to developing personalized AI-driven programs that assist individuals in their journey towards self-discovery, the fusion of psychology and technology holds immense potential in redefining how we understand and foster individuation.

The future landscape also presents a continued evolution of the societal and cultural impacts on individuation. As global interconnectedness expands, there is a heightened awareness of diverse belief systems, cultural practices, and narratives. This intercultural exchange provides a rich tapestry for individuation experiences, allowing individuals to engage with a broader spectrum of archetypal energies and mythic motifs. However, this enhanced cross-cultural dialogue also necessitates a nuanced understanding of how individuation manifests within varied cultural contexts and the implications for fostering inclusive and culturally sensitive approaches to psychological development.

Another pivotal aspect of the future landscape relates to the integration of individuation principles into interdisciplinary frameworks. As the boundaries between traditional disciplines blur, there is an increasing recognition of the relevance of individuation theory in fields such as education, organizational development, healthcare, and creative arts. The emergence of transdisciplinary collaborations offers opportunities to synthesize insights from different domains and cultivate holistic approaches to individuation that acknowledge the complex interconnectedness of human experiences.

The future landscape calls for a reevaluation of the ethical considerations and responsibilities associated with facilitating individuation processes. With an emphasis on ensuring the well-being and autonomy of individuals engaging in self-exploration, ethical guidelines and standards need to be continually refined in accordance with contemporary social and technological landscapes. This requires an ongoing dialogue among practitioners, scholars, and ethicists to uphold the integrity of individuation practices while adapting to evolving ethical dilemmas and complexities inherent in the modern age.

In conclusion, as we peer into the future landscape of individuation, it becomes evident that the field stands at the precipice of transformative possibilities. By embracing technological advancements, managing cultural diversity, fostering interdisciplinary synergy, and upholding ethical rigor, the emerging trends and innovations in individuation promise to shape a paradigm that not only resonates with the zeitgeist but also enriches the depth and breadth of human psychological growth.

# LEGACY AND FUTURE DIRECTIONS OF INDIVIDUATION

## Impacts of Jung's Individuation on Modern Psychology

Jung's concept of individuation has left an indelible mark on modern psychology, permeating various theoretical frameworks and therapeutic practices. One of the most profound impacts is evident in the field of psychotherapy, where the integration of individuation principles has revolutionized approaches to understanding and treating mental health disorders. By recognizing the significance of inner transformation and the journey towards wholeness, therapists can now employ a more holistic and humanistic approach to healing. Moreover, the emphasis on integrating the shadow aspects of the self, a central tenet of individuation, has contributed to a deeper comprehension of psychopathology and unconscious conflicts, thereby enhancing the efficacy of therapeutic interventions. As a result, contemporary therapeutic modalities such as Jungian therapy, existential therapy, and integrative psychotherapy have emerged, with their foundations deeply rooted in the principles of individuation.

The influence of Jung's individuation extends beyond clinical applications and permeates academic scholarship and research endeavors within the field of psychology. The multifaceted nature of individuation has stimulated diverse areas of inquiry, ranging from the exploration of archetypal symbolism, mythic narratives, and cultural manifestations of the collective unconscious, to the examination of the psychospiritual dimensions of human development. This expansive scope has not only broadened the horizons of psychological inquiry but has also engendered fruitful dialogues across disciplines such as anthropology, religious studies, and philosophy. The interdisciplinary collaborations that have arisen from this synergy have led to groundbreaking insights into the universality of human experience, identity formation, and consciousness evolution, enriching our understanding of the human psyche and its complex dynamics.

The advent of advancements in cognitive neuroscience and neuropsychology has facilitated the empirical examination of various aspects of individuation, offering neurobiological correlates that corroborate and elucidate Jung's conceptual framework. By employing neuroimaging techniques and psychophysiological measurements, researchers have begun to unveil the neural substrates and cognitive processes underpinning phenomena such as archetypal imagery, symbolic cognition, and the integration of unconscious material, shedding light on the neural mechanisms that underlie transformative experiences central to the individuation process.

### Interdisciplinary Influences and Collaborations

The intersection of psychology, philosophy, anthropology, and various other fields has enriched the discourse on individuation, leading to profound insights and innovative approaches. Through interdisciplinary collaborations, scholars and practitioners have been able to expand the contextual boundaries of individuation, thereby enhancing its relevance and applicability across diverse domains. This synthesis of knowledge has allowed for a more holistic and nuanced comprehension of individuation, reflecting a deep appreciation for the complexity of human development and identity formation.

In studying the interdisciplinary influences on individuation, it becomes evident that the contributions from different fields have contributed to a more comprehensive and multifaceted understanding of the concept. For instance, the incorporation of anthropological perspectives has shed light on the cultural variations and universality of individuation processes, emphasizing the impact of societal norms and traditions on an individual's journey towards wholeness. Likewise, philosophical inquiries into the nature of selfhood and consciousness have enriched the theoretical underpinnings of individuation, fostering deeper reflections on the ontological and epistemological dimensions of the self. These diverse influences have not only broadened the scope of individuation but have also prompted critical examinations of its practical implications in various professional contexts.

Interdisciplinary collaborations have propelled the evolution of therapeutic interventions and research methodologies related to individuation. The integration of neuroscientific findings, for example, has facilitated a deeper exploration of the neural correlates of individuation, offering empirical support for the psychological processes involved. This intersection has paved the way for neuro-psychoanalytic approaches that provide a bridge between biological mechanisms and psychodynamic conceptualizations, presenting new avenues for understanding and addressing individual differences in the pursuit of self-realization.

Collaborative efforts with experts in art, literature, and expressive therapies have illuminated the symbolic and creative dimensions of individuation, highlighting the significance of imagery, metaphor, and narrative in the individuation journey. The incorporation of these artistic and imaginative modalities has expanded the repertoire of therapeutic tools, offering individuals alternative means of engaging with their unconscious and integrating transformative experiences. Additionally, the advent of digital technologies has fostered innovative platforms for self-exploration and personal development, providing accessible resources for individuals to embark on their individuation quests.

### Technological Advancements and Individuation Studies

With the proliferation of digital tools, researchers and practitioners now have access to innovative methods for gathering, analyzing, and interpreting data related to individuation processes. One notable area of advancement is in the field of neuroimaging techniques, such as functional magnetic resonance imaging (fMRI) and electroencephalography (EEG), which allow for unprecedented insights into the neural correlates of individuation experiences. These technologies enable researchers to track brain activity patterns associated with the emergence of archetypal symbols, the integration of unconscious content, and the stages of personal transformation. Moreover, the utilization of virtual reality (VR) environments has revolutionized the way individuals can immerse themselves in symbolic scenarios and explore the depths of their own psyches. By leveraging VR, therapists can facilitate immersive experiences that aid in the exploration and integration of unconscious material, thereby enhancing the individuation journey for their clients. Additionally, the digital landscape has facilitated the development of sophisticated computational models and algorithms that can analyze large datasets to identify patterns and trends in individuation narratives and processes. Natural language processing (NLP) and machine learning techniques are being applied to analyze textual data from personal narratives, dreams, and therapeutic sessions, shedding light on the semantic structures and transformative themes inherent in the individuation process. Furthermore, the burgeoning field of virtual counseling and teletherapy platforms has expanded access to individuation-oriented interventions, transcending geographic, temporal, and logistical barriers. Through secure digital interfaces, individuals can engage in therapeutic encounters that support their quest for personal wholeness and self-realization. The confluence of technology and individuation studies presents an exciting frontier for the integration of empirical research, experiential exploration, and clinical applications in the pursuit of understanding and fostering the process of individuation.

### Future Research Directions and Potential Studies

As the field of Jungian psychology continues to evolve, it is imperative to identify and prioritize future research directions and potential studies that can further enrich our understanding of individuation. One promising avenue for exploration is the intersection of technology and psychological research, particularly in leveraging advanced data analytics and artificial intelligence to analyze patterns of individuation across diverse populations. By harnessing big data and innovative technological tools, researchers can gain deeper insights into the universal aspects of individuation while also acknowledging its culturally contingent nuances.

In addition, future studies could delve into the cross-cultural applicability of Jung's concept of individuation. Exploring how different cultural frameworks may influence the manifestations and interpretations of individuation processes can provide invaluable contributions to the global discourse on human development. This necessitates engaging with indigenous knowledge systems, diverse spiritual practices, and socio-historical contexts to unveil the universal and culturally specific dimensions of individuation.

Further research could also investigate the implications of individuation within marginalized or underrepresented communities, shedding light on how individuals from various sociocultural backgrounds undertake the journey towards self-realization. Such studies would offer crucial insights into the intersectionality of identity and individuation, amplifying voices that have historically been overlooked in mainstream psychological literature.

There is ample scope for longitudinal studies that track the long-term effects of individuation on individual well-being, resilience, and societal contributions. These investigations can elucidate the enduring impact of individuation across different stages of life and its correlation with mental health outcomes, interpersonal relationships, and occupational fulfillment. Longitudinal research holds the potential to validate the transformative power of individuation and guide interventions that promote holistic growth and flourishing.

Lastly, the exploration of integrative approaches that synthesize Jung's concepts of individuation with advancements in psychotherapy, mindfulness practices, and neuroscientific findings presents a compelling area for future inquiry. By bridging interdisciplinary perspectives, researchers can uncover synergistic pathways for facilitating individuation and enriching therapeutic modalities, thus fostering a more comprehensive understanding of human consciousness and potential.

## Global Perspectives

In examining Eastern cultures such as China and India, we encounter profound philosophical traditions that align closely with the core ideals of individuation. Concepts like Taoist harmony or the Hindu notion of self-realization bear striking similarities to Jung's exploration of integration and self-discovery. Delving deeper, we uncover how these cultures cultivate the process of individuation through spiritual practices, meditation, and the pursuit of inner balance and enlightenment.

Turning our focus to indigenous traditions, we encounter a rich tapestry of rituals and rites of passage that mirror the transformative journey central to individuation. From the vision quests of Native American tribes to the initiation ceremonies of African tribes, these traditions underscore the universal significance of self-awareness and personal growth across disparate cultural landscapes.

In the Western world, the impact of individuation is discernible in literature, art, and popular culture. From the existentialist philosophies of Europe to the profound symbolism in Renaissance paintings, the quest for individuation permeates the fabric of Western civilization. Moreover, contemporary movements such as multiculturalism and globalization have facilitated an exchange of ideas and practices, fostering a more inclusive approach to individuation that embraces diverse cultural narratives.

It is essential to acknowledge the challenges posed by cultural interpretations of individuation. While certain cultural paradigms may resonate harmoniously with Jung's concepts, others may present conflicting perspectives or divergent pathways to self-realization. Managing these cultural complexities requires a nuanced understanding of the contextual influences that shape individual and collective psyches, as well as an appreciation for the dynamic interplay between cultural norms and psychological development.

### Challenges and Limitations in Contemporary Contexts

As Jung's concept of individuation continues to permeate contemporary psychology, it encounters a myriad of challenges and limitations inherent in the diverse sociocultural landscape of the modern world. One of the primary challenges lies in reconciling the universality of Jungian archetypes and the collective unconscious with the unique cultural meanings and symbols present in different societies. While the core principles of individuation may resonate across cultures, variations in symbolic language and cultural norms necessitate a nuanced approach to its application.

The rapid evolution of technology presents both opportunities and challenges for the study and practice of individuation. The digital age has altered the nature of human interaction, potentially impacting the collective unconscious and the way archetypes manifest in contemporary individuals. Thus, understanding and adapting Jung's concepts in the context of digital communication, virtual reality, and social media pose significant challenges for scholars and practitioners.

The intersection of individuation with emerging psychological theories introduces complexities that demand critical examination. Integrating Jung's framework with contemporary theories such as positive psychology, neurobiology, and cognitive science requires careful consideration of the synergies and tensions between these paradigms. Additionally, ethical considerations regarding the application of individuation within therapeutic settings and the potential commodification of the individuation process in consumer culture underscore the need for vigilance amidst burgeoning interest in Jungian principles.

Another notable area of contention pertains to the tension between individual agency and societal influences in the pursuit of individuation. In an increasingly interconnected global society, individuals maneuver through complex webs of socio-political dynamics and cultural expectations, posing fundamental questions about the nature of individuation within the broader context of social systems. Moreover, disparities in access to resources and education create significant barriers to individuation, raising profound ethical dilemmas concerning equal opportunities for personal growth and self-realization.

### Integration with Emerging Psychological Theories

As the field of psychology continues to evolve, the integration of Jung's concept of individuation with emerging psychological theories has become a topic of increasing interest and importance. One area of focus involves the fusion of Jung's archetypal theory with contemporary cognitive psychology. Scholars are delving into the exploration of how universal symbols and archetypes, as proposed by Jung, can be correlated with cognitive processes such as perception, memory, and problem-solving. By examining the influence of archetypes on information processing, researchers aim to shed light on the deep-rooted impact of these symbolic representations on the human psyche and behavior.

The amalgamation of Jungian concepts with positive psychology has garnered significant attention. Positive psychology emphasizes strengths, virtues, and optimal functioning, aligning closely with Jung's emphasis on self-realization and wholeness. By synergizing these two perspectives, psychologists are exploring how the pursuit of individuation contributes to life satisfaction, meaning, and flourishing. This integration offers promising avenues for promoting mental well-being and personal growth in individuals and communities.

Additionally, the burgeoning field of neuroscience has sparked interdisciplinary inquiries into the neurological underpinnings of individuation. Psychologists collaborating with neuroscientists are investigating the neural correlates of individuation experiences, including the interplay of neurotransmitters, brain regions, and connectivity patterns. This interdisciplinary approach holds the potential to illuminate the biological foundations of self-discovery and identity formation, providing a comprehensive understanding of individuation from both psychological and neuroscientific standpoints.

The integration of Jungian psychology with existential psychotherapy has opened new horizons for therapeutic applications. By incorporating existential themes of meaning, authenticity, and mortality anxiety into the framework of individuation, practitioners are developing innovative interventions that address the fundamental existential concerns of individuals within the context of their individuation journeys. This integration underscores the relevance of Jung's ideas in the sphere of contemporary psychotherapeutic practices, offering profound insights into the human experience and psychological well-being.

## The Role of Individuation in Personal Development

One of the key aspects of individuation is the recognition and acceptance of the shadow – the repressed or disowned aspects of the self. By acknowledging and integrating these shadow elements, individuals can transcend inner conflicts and achieve a greater wholeness. Moreover, individuation involves the discovery and cultivation of the persona – the social mask that individuals present to the world. By understanding the roles and expectations imposed by society, individuals can strive towards authenticity and genuine self-expression.

The process of individuation encourages individuals to engage with their anima (the feminine aspect within men) or animus (the masculine aspect within women), fostering a harmonious integration of gender-related traits. Through this integration, individuals seek to strike a balance between opposing qualities, leading to a more holistic and balanced psyche. Additionally, individuation empowers individuals to embrace encounters with the Self, representing the archetypal center of the personality and the ultimate goal of the individuation process.

In personal development, individuation serves as a catalyst for transformative experiences and psychological maturation. It enables individuals to break free from societal conditioning and cultivate a strong sense of autonomy and purpose. By engaging in a process of self-exploration and inner dialogue, individuals can face existential challenges, confront existential dilemmas, and emerge with a renewed sense of meaning and direction in life.

Ultimately, the role of individuation in personal development extends beyond mere self-improvement; it encompasses a profound journey towards self-realization and the actualization of one's innate potential. By embracing the complexities of the psyche and embracing the individuation process, individuals can unlock new dimensions of personal growth, leading to a life rich with authenticity, fulfillment, and profound meaning.

## JUNG'S 50 QUOTES ON THE THEORY OF INDIVIDUATION

### On the Core of Individuation

"Individuation means becoming an 'in-dividual,' and, in so far as 'individuality' embraces our innermost, last, and incomparable uniqueness, it also implies becoming one's own self."

"Individuation is the process by which a person becomes a psychological 'in-dividual,' that is, a separate, indivisible unity or whole."

"The privilege of a lifetime is to become who you truly are."

"What you are is what you have always been. What you are to be is what you do now."

"The goal of the individuation process is the synthesis of the self."

"Individuation is a process of differentiation, having for its goal the development of the individual personality."

### On the Shadow

"One does not become enlightened by imagining figures of light, but by making the darkness conscious."

"To confront a person with his shadow is to show him his own light."

"The shadow is a moral problem that challenges the whole ego-personality."

"Knowing your own darkness is the best method for dealing with the darkness of other people."

"The shadow is that hidden, repressed, for the most part inferior and guilt-laden personality whose ultimate ramifications reach back into the sphere of our animal ancestors."

### On the Persona

"The persona is that which in reality one is not, but which oneself and others think one is."

"The persona is a kind of mask, designed on the one hand to make a definite impression upon others, and on the other to conceal the true nature of the individual."

"Every calling or profession has its own characteristic persona."

"It is not real when we assume a pose and mask of personality; it is a compromise between individual and society."

### On the Anima & Animus

"The anima is a personification of all feminine psychological tendencies within a man, the archetypal feminine symbolism within his unconscious."

"The animus is the deposit, as it were, of all woman's ancestral experiences of man—and not only that, he also brings to light creative qualities in a woman."

"The anima and animus are both mediators between the conscious and the unconscious."

"The encounter with the shadow is the 'apprentice-piece' in the individual's development… with the anima, it is the 'masterpiece.'"

"The integration of the anima and animus requires confrontation, not repression."

## On the Self & Wholeness

"The self is not only the center but also the whole circumference which embraces both conscious and unconscious; it is the center of this totality, just as the ego is the center of consciousness."

"The self is our life's goal, for it is the completest expression of that fateful combination we call individuality."

"Wholeness is not achieved by cutting off a portion of one's being, but by integration of the contraries."

"Only the paradox comes anywhere near to comprehending the fullness of life."

"The self is a quantity that is supraordinate to the conscious ego. It embraces not only the conscious but also the unconscious psyche."

## On the Unconscious

"The unconscious is not just evil by nature; it is also the source of the highest good."

"Until you make the unconscious conscious, it will direct your life and you will call it fate."

"The unconscious is the matrix out of which consciousness grows."

"There is no coming to consciousness without pain."

"Who looks outside, dreams; who looks inside, awakes."

## On the Path of Individuation

"The way is not straight but spiral."

"There is no linear evolution; there is only a circumambulation of the self."

"In each of us there is another whom we do not know."

"Your visions will become clear only when you can look into your own heart."

"Loneliness does not come from having no people around you, but from being unable to communicate the things that seem important to you."

"Everything that irritates us about others can lead us to an understanding of ourselves."

## On Transformation and Growth

"The most terrifying thing is to accept oneself completely."

"We cannot change anything unless we accept it."

"I am not what happened to me, I am what I choose to become."

"In all chaos there is a cosmos, in all disorder a secret order."

"The greatest and most important problems of life are all fundamentally insoluble. They can never be solved but only outgrown."

## On Archetypes & Symbols

"Archetypes are the living system of reactions and aptitudes that determine the individual's life in invisible ways."

"The symbols of the self arise in the depths of the body."

"The dream is a little hidden door in the innermost and most secret recesses of the soul."

"The collective unconscious contains the whole spiritual heritage of mankind's evolution born anew in the brain structure of every individual."

**On the Spiritual Dimension of Individuation**

"The experience of the self is always a defeat for the ego."

"Man's task is to become conscious of the contents that press upward from the unconscious."

"The individuation process brings into consciousness all the aspects of the human psyche, and this process is the real source of religious experience."

"A complete life, a life truly lived, is one that has faced its own depths."

"He who looks within awakens the divine."

www.ingramcontent.com/pod-product-compliance
Lightning Source LLC
LaVergne TN
LVHW022041200926
848481LV00003B/735
* 9 7 9 8 2 3 2 2 2 4 4 9 3 *